T0289520

About Island Press

Since 1984, the nonprofit organization Island Press has been stimulating, shaping, and communicating ideas that are essential for solving environmental problems worldwide. With more than 1,000 titles in print and some 30 new releases each year, we are the nation's leading publisher on environmental issues. We identify innovative thinkers and emerging trends in the environmental field. We work with world-renowned experts and authors to develop cross-disciplinary solutions to environmental challenges.

Island Press designs and executes educational campaigns, in conjunction with our authors, to communicate their critical messages in print, in person, and online using the latest technologies, innovative programs, and the media. Our goal is to reach targeted audiences—scientists, policy makers, environmental advocates, urban planners, the media, and concerned citizens—with information that can be used to create the framework for long-term ecological health and human well-being.

Island Press gratefully acknowledges major support from The Bobolink Foundation, Caldera Foundation, The Curtis and Edith Munson Foundation, The Forrest C. and Frances H. Lattner Foundation, The JPB Foundation, The Kresge Foundation, The Summit Charitable Foundation, Inc., and many other generous organizations and individuals.

The opinions expressed in this book are those of the author(s) and do not necessarily reflect the views of our supporters.

Vacant to Vibrant

Vacant to Vibrant

Creating Successful Green Infrastructure Networks

Sandra L. Albro

ISLANDPRESS

Washington | Covelo | London

Library of Congress Control Number: 2018966625

All Island Press books are printed on environmentally responsible materials.

Manufactured in the United States of America
10 9 8 7 6 5 4 3 2 1

Keywords: Buffalo (New York), Cleveland (Ohio), combined sewer output, community engagement, curb cut, demographics, downspout disconnect, equity, Hardest Hit Funds, health, Gary (Indiana), GIS, Great Lakes, green infrastructure, legacy cities, maintenance, native plants, neighborhood stabilization, People United for Sustainable Housing, post-industrial city, rain garden, recreation, safety, shrinking cities, social justice, stewardship, stormwater management, stormwater runoff, urban planning, vacant lot, Vacant to Vibrant, water quality, workforce development

Contents

Introduction

In 2012, three staff members of the Cleveland Botanical Garden took a tour of Great Lakes cities to better understand how those cities were repurposing vacant lots. After being involved with urban farming for two decades, we had witnessed firsthand how urban farms improved the social fabric of neighborhoods. Given the demands of urban farming, however, and the growing inventories of vacant lots in Cleveland and other cities around the Great Lakes, we became interested in other ways to return vacant lots to productive use. Were there ways to repurpose vacant land that were less expensive and less labor intensive than urban agriculture, but that could still help address decades of environmental degradation and urban decline?

Lessons from Urban Farming
In Cleveland, the botanical garden had been part of a growing urban farming movement that was also present in Milwaukee, Chicago, Detroit, and other cities. Over 20 years, the botanical garden's Green Corps urban farming program for youth had expanded from one urban farm to six, giving up to 90 high school students per summer work experience in growing, harvesting, and selling fresh produce in parts of the city where affordable fresh food was hard to come by. It was clear from our experience in cultivating these vacant lots that farming created valuable life experiences for youth. It was also clear that farms had become community assets, removing eyesores and restoring productivity to vacant land. The farms had become places to congregate—to pass the time when school was out, to buy produce, or to just stand and watch food being grown.

Aside from the obvious benefits of urban agriculture, we suspected that the farms were providing unseen benefits too. Researchers from The Ohio State University began studying beneficial insects found on urban farms and community gardens in

Cleveland in 2009. They found that the gardens provided habitat for many varieties of bees, ants, and predatory (beneficial) wasps; however, so did vacant lots, to a
sometimes surprising degree.[1]

Another study, from Oberlin College, showed that urban farms and community
gardens provided clear economic benefit to communities, boosting values of nearby
properties by 3.5 percent.[2] The problem was that, in these communities, 3.5 percent
of $2,500 (for an average vacant lot) or $15,000 (for a single-family home) was not
enough wealth to help stabilize declining neighborhoods.

In spite of the benefits of urban farms, urban farming is hard work. Restoring urban
soils to productive use is tough manual labor, requiring a large input of food waste,
animal manure, compost, yard clippings, and paper waste to restore organic matter and
water-holding capacity to a point where the soil can support food crops.[3] As in most
farming, profit margins in urban farming are low, making financial sustainability difficult. While urban farming educational programs are often supported by grant dollars,
private farmers find it difficult to support themselves on the income generated by urban
agriculture. Lower productivity of urban soil means that plants are harder to grow; prof-
its are consumed by costs for leasing land, watering plants, and protecting assets.

At the botanical garden, with experience in urban farming came expertise in
repurposing vacant land. Community members started to approach us with questions about how to put their own urban greening plans into motion. At the same
time, we recognized that urban farming alone could not reach the scale necessary to
repurpose thousands of vacant parcels, especially as demolition efforts were acceler-
ating in the wake of the foreclosure crisis. In places that were not suitable for urban
farming, what other land uses could build social and environmental capital? How
could the social justice lens of the urban farming movement extend the reach of
urban environmental projects? Considering the large amounts of time, labor, and
money needed for urban farming, we began looking for other ways to repurpose
vacant lots that would provide similar social and environmental benefits to neighborhoods. We set out on a driving tour that led us from Cleveland to both ends of
the Great Lakes basin—Chicago and Milwaukee to the west, and Buffalo and Toronto
to the east—to plan what form a new project might take.

Vacant Lots as Green Stormwater Infrastructure
We observed several similarities among US Great Lakes cities on our driving tour.
Many cities were several decades into population loss. Land bank legislation in
the mid-2000s had streamlined the clearing of abandoned houses and the creation
of vacant land in Michigan and Ohio. When the federal Hardest Hit Fund was

established in 2010, some of those land banks were able to effectively capture funding to significantly ramp up demolition efforts. Cities were starting to grapple with new problems caused by high densities of vacant lots, still seen as "blight."

At the same time that cities were starting to contend with large quantities of vacant land, they faced a growing, palpable threat of consent decrees by the US Environmental Protection Agency (USEPA), which was ramping up efforts to use the Clean Water Act to compel cities to make significant upgrades to their sewer systems. This strategy was shaping up to be an effective way to reduce the 24 billion gallons per year of untreated combined sewer overflow into the Great Lakes. In 2010, the Northeast Ohio Regional Sewer District, whose service area includes Cleveland, had just negotiated the first consent decree to allow green stormwater infrastructure to count toward acceptable sewer improvements. This, in addition to demonstrated success in other parts of the country, helped pique regional interest in green stormwater infrastructure.

Although many cities were struggling under the dual weight of required infrastructure updates and land vacancy, while also dealing with shrinking tax bases, in 2010 there was little overlap in solutions to the two problems. Cities such as Milwaukee and Chicago, which were early adopters of green infrastructure in the region, were implementing it mostly in wealthier neighborhoods, away from areas with high land vacancy. In addition, the types of green stormwater infrastructure being installed were large and imposing, with high costs. These large retention or detention basins were often paired with other capital improvements, such as sewer separation and street resurfacing, to maximize the surface area that would drain to each stormwater management project. Such approaches were limited to locations where it was possible to aggregate a number of adjacent parcels. Additionally, because of skepticism about the ability of green infrastructure to hold and clean stormwater, in many cases green stormwater best management practices were still connected to sewer systems via overflows. Around the same time, researchers at USEPA and US Geological Survey had undertaken studies on the permeability of small residential vacant lots and were finding that they could absorb more stormwater than expected.[4]

New Uses for Vacant Land

This book describes our insights gained over the past seven years of developing Vacant to Vibrant, a project to convert small, vacant parcels to "stormwater parks"—pocket parks containing stormwater control measures—to address three problems affecting post-industrial cities—excess vacant land, aging sewer infrastructure, and declining neighborhoods. While Vacant to Vibrant set out to address a confluence of problems that are found in older US manufacturing cities, our hope is that its lessons will prove useful for implementation of similar projects in any city or neighborhood that is looking for solutions to any of these problems.

Drawing on the collective experience of a diverse project team that spanned three cities, this book is written for urban greening practitioners of all stripes, from designers and implementers to laborers and policymakers. It presents a variety of findings that cover the life span of an urban greening project. We honestly describe both the successful outcomes and the shortcomings, because both of these yielded useful lessons. Beyond simple replication of the projects, we hope that the processes, lessons, and design plans that we describe here will be built and improved upon.

Chapters 1 and 2 will provide an overview of the processes that led to the current state of post-industrial cities in the US: the creation of abundant urban vacant land, aging sewer and stormwater infrastructure in need of innovation to address future climate and population threats, and urban neighborhoods that still bear witness to the economic and social conditions that built them. Through planning, implementing, and maintaining stormwater parks across three cities, Vacant to Vibrant attempted to tackle systemic barriers to reusing urban vacant land as green infrastructure. In this book, we describe lessons we learned that could be applied to many types of urban greening projects.

Chapter 2 provides an example of the kind of background research that can inform project implementation—even if it seems far afield from the practicalities of green infrastructure—so that site selection, community outreach, and project design can be grounded in the unique attributes of a place. It explores social dynamics that built and, later, dismantled urban neighborhoods that fed manufacturing plants in the three Vacant to Vibrant cities. Chapters 3 and 4 delve into details of the approach that Vacant to Vibrant took to planning and building urban greening projects to address cities' needs for vacant land use, stormwater management, and neighborhood stabilization. Chapter 5 discusses performance of projects, difficult lessons about maintenance, and how to anticipate challenges. Finally, Chapter 6 discusses remaining hurdles to taking urban greening projects to the scale of infrastructure and the potential for vacant lots to form expansive green infrastructure networks.

The scale of urban green space that will be required to build healthier urban communities and protect them from future economic and environmental threats is much too large for one approach. Ultimately, Vacant to Vibrant is about finding potential in overlooked places and reexamining how, and for whom, urban green space can be built to last.

1

Green Stormwater Infrastructure on Vacant Lots

The benefits that urban green space provides to cities have been well documented. It reduces expenditures for vital services such as air filtration, stormwater management, and temperature regulation.[1] Urban green space adds value to nearby properties, increases commerce, and reduces violent crime. It improves human health outcomes[2] by reducing stress,[3] encouraging exercise,[4] and reducing illness and death from respiratory disease. The Vacant to Vibrant project was inspired to bring these benefits to areas where they could assist with neighborhood stabilization. We created a project to build urban green space on small vacant parcels in three post-industrial cities with the goal of improving the environmental and social fabric of neighborhoods.

Vacant to Vibrant began as a hashtag, #vacant2vibrant, used to organize conversations over a series of interdisciplinary meetings in 2009 and 2010.[5] Dozens of professionals from city government, sewer/stormwater authorities, and urban greening organizations from 11 Great Lakes cities met to characterize shared problems that were emerging as state and federal monies were being invested in blight removal and demolition of abandoned buildings, creating growing catalogs of vacant lots. We wanted to understand existing vacant land reuse efforts and explore how these might complement environmental initiatives that were taking place in the same cities.

From this process, the group identified three areas of need that were common to many urban areas in the Great Lakes region:

- Large quantities of vacant land that were unproductive and expensive to maintain

- Outdated sewer systems that were creating a need for better stormwater management in the face of a changing climate
- Neighborhoods that had weathered the environmental and social effects of decades of industrial decline

Vacant to Vibrant drew upon innovative vacant land reuse work that had been undertaken in many places around the US, such as pocket parks, green stormwater infrastructure, urban farming, and "clean-and-green" neighborhood stabilization projects. While its primary focus was finding a way to use vacant lots to benefit the Great Lakes ecosystem, Vacant to Vibrant differed from many environmental projects that were being implemented at the time in its equal emphasis on the social and the environmental needs of urban neighborhoods. Its effort to combine vacant land reuse, green stormwater infrastructure, and neighborhood revitalization tested whether land use strategies could be stacked within the small footprint of a single lot.

The project included beautification of three vacant parcels in one neighborhood in each of three Great Lakes cities—Gary, Indiana; Cleveland, Ohio; and Buffalo, New York. We targeted declining neighborhoods that could benefit from stabilization and set out to develop modest urban greening approaches that were customized to the needs of those neighborhoods. Rain gardens were added to each parcel, as well as landscaping or equipment that supported a recreational use for residents. The type of recreation varied from very passive, such as walking, bird-watching, or picnicking, to more active, such as handball or active play. Where possible, flower beds and low-maintenance plants replaced lawn to reduce mowing requirements and add habitat. In the interest of replicability, we strived for modest projects with installation costs ranging from $7,000 to $35,000 (average: $18,000) over nine installations.

This approach contrasted with large stormwater management projects that were being undertaken in Milwaukee, Chicago, and Cleveland on aggregated vacant land. It also contrasted with green streets and smaller stormwater management projects that were being constructed in stable or gentrifying neighborhoods in many cities throughout the US. Beyond the construction of projects themselves, Vacant to Vibrant was an attempt to document processes and lessons that could help lead to systemic change—change that would be necessary if cities want to grow green stormwater control up to the level of "infrastructure." The three cities provided separate examples of how manufacturing cities are grappling with adapting old systems to new, green technology.

In this chapter, we explore how population loss that created thousands of acres of vacant land also contributed to letting underlying urban infrastructure fall out of date. As a result, cities with a shrinking base of tax- and ratepayers are contending with large sewer infrastructure updates for regulatory compliance. Examining these two problems in tandem may suggest where and what form joint solutions might take to repurpose vacant lots for the benefit of environmental quality.

Excess Urban Vacant Land

In the late 19th and early 20th centuries, US cities boomed with the spread of industrialization. Near the Great Lakes, where expansive bodies of freshwater fueled production and provided access to international shipping routes, cities rapidly expanded under steel and manufacturing. Large cities annexed smaller towns and undeveloped land to support an influx of residents from the East, rural areas, and abroad. They laid roads, sewers, and other infrastructure in an expanding urban grid. When rivers and beaches blackened and caught fire, their loss was a cost of progress.

After the demands of World War II ended and manufacturing slowed in the region, city economies began shifting away from heavy industry. On the Canadian side, early economic diversification to embrace light industry, tech, and service sectors spurred population growth in the 1970s that continues to this day.[6] A short drive across the border into Detroit or Buffalo, however, shows that Great Lakes cities on the US side did not adapt as quickly. Job loss caused by automation and imports was exacerbated by US racial politics. Desegregation of schools and neighborhoods fed white flight and urban sprawl that gutted downtowns and permanently altered the demographics of urban neighborhoods.

Many American post-industrial cities continued to lose population from the 1960s onward. In some cities, the pattern of population loss was widespread across most of their land area (Detroit, Gary, Flint). In other places, population loss and disinvestment were concentrated in some neighborhoods, while other areas continued to grow (Chicago, Philadelphia, New York). In the 1990s, it was common to see a distribution of regional population in a doughnut shape around cities, with thriving suburban areas surrounding decaying urban cores.[7] Today, as population loss slows, cities are receiving an influx of younger, highly educated residents, so that downtown growth and continued suburban development now sandwich decaying urban neighborhoods. In development hot spots, problems of urban decay are now being replaced with problems of gentrification. Today, rather than thinking of urban shrinkage as a permanent phenomenon, it is thought that shrinkage is one phase of the urban life cycle that precedes growth.[8]

Cities positioned near the Great Lakes have been particularly affected by vacancy due to regional industrial decline since the 1970s, with 14 of the 20 largest cities experiencing population loss of 15 to 45 percent over 40 years.[9] How this population loss scales with the quantity of vacant land depends on cities' capacity to undertake large-scale demolition efforts—some cities have had more access to resources for demolition than others. Vacant land is not unique to cities that have gone through decades of depopulation, however. Land vacancy exists in a majority of cities throughout the US,[10] such as cities that have gone through rapid expansion, or cities where geography or policy has allowed sprawl to go unchecked. Aside from house demolition, other conditions that create vacant land include soil contamination, undevelopable slopes, and oddly shaped parcels left by highways and urban sprawl. Finding productive ways to reuse vacant land is of interest to a variety of countries in Europe and Asia, where slower population and economic growth rates, deindustrialization, suburbanization, and globalization have contributed to population loss in cities. As in parts of the US, these conditions abroad have created urban areas that are contending with environmental quality problems, outdated infrastructure, and land vacancy.[11]

Development of small residential parcels during periods of growth, followed by widespread property abandonment, foreclosure, and demolition of vacant structures during industrial decline, has resulted in hundreds or thousands of vacant parcels per city in the Midwest and northeast regions (figure 1-1[12]). Vacancy can occur as large parcels that often bear the contamination of past industrial use, but urban vacant land more commonly takes the form of small residential or commercial parcels that dot street corners and are sandwiched between homes. Due to the piecemeal nature of abandonment and demolition, vacant lots are usually unconnected from one another except in neighborhoods that have had very high rates of population loss (for example, in Cleveland, 85 percent of vacant land exists as three or fewer contiguous parcels, and more than 96 percent of vacant land aggregates are smaller than 0.2 hectares in size). The separation of vacant lots in space and in time—in addition to varied land use histories, sheer number, and the limited resources of shrinking cities—have made it difficult to put vacant lots into productive use.

With population and/or economic stability returning to manufacturing cities, planning for growth has taken on a tone of increased urgency and realism. Smaller, single-company manufacturing cities, such as Flint, Michigan, and Youngstown, Ohio, are planning to shrink urban infrastructure to match projections that population will remain smaller in the long run. Most larger cities shy away from shrinkage as an overt strategy, however, viewing it as being unflattering or pessimistic. These cities are cautiously envisioning what vibrant futures might look like.

In particular, shrinking cities that are situated near abundant freshwater are

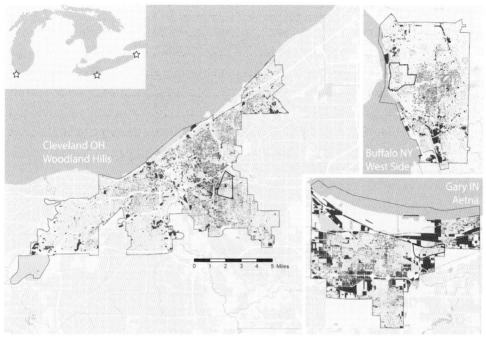

Figure 1-1. Like many post-industrial cities that have had significant population loss over the past several decades, the three Vacant to Vibrant cities in this book—Cleveland, Ohio; Buffalo, New York; and Gary, Indiana—have an abundance of urban vacant land. Data sources: NEOCANDO and City of Cleveland, Cities of Buffalo and Gary, Esri.

poised for future growth. There is renewed interest in restoring the rivers and lakes that once made eastern cities attractive to manufacturing, while water scarcity predictions for the Southwest and western US have underscored the potential of abundant clean water for future economic growth. These cities are rediscovering clean water as an asset. On shore, nostalgia for earlier times has also rekindled a longing to reclaim "forest cities," a nickname that several cities in North America (Cleveland, Ohio; Rockford, Illinois; London, Ontario, Canada; Portland, Maine; and Middletown, Connecticut) once shared. Environmental compliance issues and climate uncertainty are spurring planning that views water and trees through the lens of climate resilience.

Although[13] generally considered "blight," high rates of urban land vacancy in US post-industrial cities present an opportunity for new, climate-smart patterns of urban redevelopment. On the flip side of manufacturing loss is an opportunity for post-industrial cities to reinvent themselves as vibrant urban areas, where clean, green space serves the economy, residents, and the environment.

Vacant Land as Urban Green Space

In this time of abundant vacant land, "legacy" cities have a window of opportunity to shift away from previous patterns of development by intentionally planning for vacant parcels that will not be rebuilt. Instead, they can re-create themselves as greener cities that are more resilient to future threats by planning for urban green space that is more densely and equitably distributed. By learning from cities that have grown too quickly or densely, they can avoid future costs and problems associated with trying to retrofit green space into densely populated areas.

Managing vacant parcels is often seen as a temporary problem—when there is demand for property for tax-generating land uses again, planners will no longer be asking what vacant parcels are good for. The larger point of vacant land management goes beyond finding interim uses for parcels until they can be redeveloped; it extends to helping determine the best long-term use for parcels within a vibrant city from among a wide array of possibilities. This includes developing criteria for how parcels should be redeveloped or whether they should be redeveloped at all. By describing the full suite of benefits that urban green space provides, including ecological and social benefits, and the monetary value of those benefits, urban greening practitioners can incorporate informed decision making into the planning process for redevelopment. Good policy will be crucial to ensure that adequate green space is preserved for neighborhoods as parcels are acquired and developed one at a time, all over the city, across decades.

While green infrastructure has been embraced in regions such as the Pacific Northwest, manufacturing cities tend to prefer the certainty of traditional engineering solutions. Extensive greening in the urban core also conflicts with the original development patterns of these cities—modest houses in densely packed neighborhoods that did not contain much urban green space. However, abundant vacant land resources and philanthropic interest in green jobs are pushing blue-collar urban areas to explore the potential in green infrastructure.

The Slavic Village neighborhood in Cleveland is a good illustration of development patterns that persisted in industrial cities into the 1950s. Narrow 40- by 100-foot parcels were built up into two- and three-story colonial houses that stretched from driveway to driveway. Detached garages, and sometimes another small house to hold family from the old country (the "mother-in-law suite"), filled the rear of the parcel. Most trees were cleared. Today approximately one-quarter of the parcels in Slavic Village are vacant, and many houses have been abandoned and condemned, awaiting conversion to vacant land through demolition.

Yet many city officials and residents, in Cleveland and elsewhere, still cling to midcentury images of crowded parcels, filled with impervious surfaces that we now know contribute to sewer flash floods that lead to overflows, as a badge of their cities' heyday. Even with clear evidence that modern development patterns should change, they continue to assume that their cities will again be healthy when every parcel is built back up to its original glory.

This idea may not be stated explicitly but can be perceived between the lines in plans that fail to preserve some vacant parcels as permanent urban green space. Many cities largely lack regulations that force the preservation or creation of urban green space, particularly in densely packed or quickly growing neighborhoods, despite a current window of opportunity to envision neighborhoods that are more equitable, walkable, and climate resilient. Many of these same cities do promote green reuse of vacant lots as a temporary holding strategy, however, and pattern books containing recipes for temporary vacant lot reuse strategies are common.[13] In its guidebook on this topic, "Temporary Urbanism: Alternative Approaches to Vacant Land," the US Department of Housing and Urban Development discusses vacant land use primarily as a way to attract investors and reiterates a common concern about vacant land projects:

> In places where temporary interventions have successfully empowered marginalized individuals and turned urban blight into a neighborhood asset, any attempt by a landowner or government authorities to reassert control over the site will likely be met with fierce resistance. . . . The risk of negative press or legal complications from such events may discourage developers from permitting temporary uses in the first place.[14]

The development of land banks has greatly improved the ability to access and aggregate abandoned parcels. A limitation of land banks is that many are only temporary holders of vacant land, by design. Both Genesee County Land Bank (Flint) and Cuyahoga Land Bank (Cleveland) hold parcels over a short period of time, either to rehab the houses and sell them, or to demolish them and pass the vacant land on to other, longer-term holding entities. In many cities that are hungry to grow their tax base, preservation of vacant parcels takes a back seat to development in neighborhoods with market demand.

But there is growing recognition of the potential held within vacant properties by some entities. Park districts are seizing the opportunity to grow their land holdings by purchasing vacant land that connects to parks, reserves, or other urban green space. In Ohio, state funding is available for that purpose (Clean Ohio Fund). Sewer authorities, under consent decree to manage stormwater and observing growing evidence of the effectiveness of green stormwater infrastructure, are purchasing vacant parcels to manage stormwater and provide access points for underground pipes.

Proposals to set aside vacant parcels for permanent preservation as urban green space are starting to appear in long-term city plans. Chicago's CitySpace Plan was among the first of these, created to raise Chicago's rank among similarly sized cities in the amount of urban green space per capita (4.13 acres per 1,000 residents, 18th of 20 in 1998).[15] As of 2012, the proposals and rationale outlined in CitySpace had sparked the preservation of an additional 1,344 acres of green space.

In Pennsylvania, Pittsburgh's 12-part, 25-year plan has an open space component, OpenSpacePGH, that details guidelines for land use and infrastructure decisions that affect the city's 30,000 vacant, distressed, and undeveloped properties.[16] The plan categorizes "opportunity lands" by 16 types of reuse potential based on parcel and surrounding characteristics. In addition, OpenSpacePGH identifies lack of adequate green space as a growing threat in neighborhoods with high market demand.

Farther east, Baltimore's Green Network Plan, in draft form in 2018, proposes to use vacant parcels to grow a system of connecting recreational spaces, trails, and urban gardens.[17] Also up for public comment in 2018 is the city of Gary's comprehensive city plan update, which proposes using vacant lots as green stormwater infrastructure to improve the quality of rivers and beaches.[18]

Stormwater Management in Cities with Aging Infrastructure

Loss of population in post-industrial cities has also created problems for aging urban infrastructure. Roads, utilities, and sewer systems all contend with, and sometimes compete for, shrinking revenue from tax- and ratepayers. Broken pipes, antiquated technology, and changes in climate patterns are creating demand for sewer updates to decrease the frequency of pollution discharges into waterways. To acknowledge the enormous cost of updating sewer systems, and to try to increase the benefits of these investments for ratepayers, green stormwater infrastructure is increasingly being considered as part of a suite of sewer system updates to manage rain and snow melt closer to where it originates.

Stormwater runoff from impervious surfaces is a main source of non-point pollution that negatively affects water quality in many US municipalities. Combined with other sources of water pollution from urban areas, including wastewater treatment plant bypasses and combined sewer overflows, these sources transmit more than 850 billion gallons of untreated water annually into waterways in the Great Lakes and northeast regions of the US, comprising 4 percent of all municipal water discharges. Urban stormwater runoff from impervious surfaces makes up another

10,000 billion gallons, or 45 percent of all municipal water discharges. (For comparison, treated wastewater equals 11,400 billion gallons, or 51 percent of municipal discharges.)[19]

Combined sewer systems[20] are present in 860 US municipalities that experienced major growth during the late 19th century,[21] when such systems were a major technological advancement against epidemics such as cholera.[22]

Regulatory Action as a Driver of Green Infrastructure

In recent years, regulatory compliance has become a growing driver of investment in green stormwater infrastructure. The US Environmental Protection Agency (USEPA) has been taking enforcement action on municipal sewer systems to improve water quality and reduce the quantity of pollution discharges into lakes, rivers, and streams since the late 1970s, ramping up in the 2000s. Enforcement action can take the form of consent decrees or other punitive measures to compel municipal sewer authorities to create long-term control plans to mitigate water pollution. Since 2009, on the recommendation of the International Joint Commission of Canada and the US, these agreements have increasingly encouraged the use of green stormwater control measures, including green roofs, rain gardens, permeable pavement, and vacant land improvements.[23]

Specific to the Great Lakes watershed are designations of Areas of Concern by the US–Canada Great Lakes Water Quality Agreement, identifying severely degraded geographic areas that negatively influence regional water quality. Forced accountability to the Clean Water Act of 1972 has pushed cities near Areas of Concern and elsewhere in the US to reevaluate their stormwater infrastructure and begin billions of dollars worth of upgrades, retrofits, and new facilities. Several cities have turned to construction of massive storage tunnels—up to 32 feet in diameter and miles long, drilled into bedrock at depths of 200 feet or more—that are designed to hold peak flow until volume can be managed by water treatment facilities. Storage tunnels of this type have been constructed in Cleveland, Detroit, Chicago, Fort Wayne, and Toledo.

Many of these cities are also exploring the use of green stormwater infrastructure to reduce the number or size of gray infrastructure projects. Green infrastructure makes use of natural systems, or engineered systems that mimic natural processes, to manage stormwater, promoting local infiltration and using plants and soil to clean, evapotranspire, or reduce water velocity and erosion.[24] (Throughout the book, "green infrastructure" is used to describe green space that has been designed to perform a specific ecological service—usually, stormwater management—while "urban green space" is used more generally to describe spaces that deliver a variety of services.) As evidence builds that green infrastructure can effectively manage stormwater runoff and confer other ecosystem benefits, long-term control plans for sewage and stormwater are increasingly including green infrastructure as part of the system updates required for compliance.

Large versus Small Green Infrastructure

The format of green stormwater infrastructure can be divided into two types: large projects that collect stormwater from many parcels and route it to a single stormwater management feature, and smaller, distributed projects that sit higher in the watershed and collect stormwater closer to where it falls. As an example of a large stormwater project, the Northeast Ohio Regional Sewer District, which includes the city of Cleveland, is constructing green stormwater infrastructure on 39 acres (including 31 acres of vacant land) to mitigate at least 500 million gallons (out of a goal of 4 billion gallons) of combined sewer overflow volume annually.[25] Their approach centers on large projects that require the aggregation of numerous vacant parcels, with the goal of improving the overall health, welfare, and socioeconomic conditions of neighborhoods by providing benefits above stormwater capture, such as improved air quality, recreational space, and removal of blighted properties.[26] In Milwaukee, the Menomonee River stormwater park incorporates pedestrian trails and waterfront access into a brownfield redevelopment site that manages stormwater from a large basin up to the level of a 100-year storm event. In Detroit, transformation of entire neighborhoods of vacant land into lakes for stormwater management has been proposed.[27]

In contrast to the large installations, a distributed stormwater management approach makes use of the most common type of urban vacant parcel—small, unconnected, formerly residential or commercial lots. While residential parcels are least likely to require expensive remediation, acquiring and aggregating many parcels can be a logistical challenge. A distributed stormwater management approach manages runoff closer to where it originates, however, so it does not require sewer separation, discharge, or associated costly infrastructure.

An advantage of distributed green infrastructure is that numerous smaller projects offer a higher level of engagement within neighborhoods, providing more interaction with residents. Research from cities that have excess land vacancy due to population loss or urban sprawl shows that urban greening projects that are tailored for stormwater management can also strengthen neighborhoods. In Philadelphia, vacant land that has been cleaned of trash and debris, greened with grass and trees, and managed as part of the Philadelphia LandCare program has lowered violent crime[28] and increased property values.[29] Additionally, green stormwater infrastructure in Philadelphia yielded reductions in public safety incidents within a half-mile radius.[30] In Baltimore and Pittsburgh, crime rates are lower in neighborhoods with more tree canopy.[31]

Challenges to Building Green Infrastructure on Vacant Lots

Despite growing evidence of the myriad benefits of green infrastructure networks, many challenges remain. A majority of vacant land reuse projects are single projects that are planned from the parcel level up. Typically, they start with a neighborhood eyesore or problem; a proposal is created for a project that will address the problem; funding is secured; and the project is built. Even for stormwater control, it is not uncommon to see green infrastructure projects planned in this way, where a parcel's position in the watershed, soil permeability, slope, and other physical attributes that affect stormwater management are not considered until later stages. A risk of this approach is that implementation costs can be out of scale with the resulting level of stormwater control.

This normal mode of operations hinders the ability to scale green stormwater projects up to the level of urban infrastructure, where cost efficiency and performance metrics guide investment decisions. A roadblock to changing the way projects are planned is difficulty in acquiring the necessary data; additionally, spatial tools, where they exist, often do not support top-down decision making. Sources for data on ownership, land use history, and physical attributes are typically scattered across multiple entities. Data access can be especially difficult for practitioners outside of local government, because some types of data, such as detailed sewer information, are considered to be sensitive. Scaling up green stormwater infrastructure will require detailed information about social and environmental attributes that can help decision makers work from all available sites down to specific parcels with desired features.

As an example of the potential impact that tools can have, urban forestry has demonstrated success in enlisting cities to set and achieve large-scale tree canopy goals via a suite of free and paid toolkits, software, and guidance documentation aimed at decision makers. These products have helped dozens of cities throughout the US understand the value of their urban canopy and create plans for growing it for the benefit of humans and the environment.[32] The demonstrated value of urban tree canopy has led to recent recommendations that tree planting and maintenance costs become part of urban health budgets, because of clear evidence that they improve public health outcomes.[33] Although these tools stop short of including parcel-level information that is specific to vacant lots, such as ownership and land use history, they make clear suggestions for where urban forest canopy is absent but possible, and they show the societal impacts that can be delivered through placement of individual trees.

Difficulty in accessing data that are necessary for informed land use decisions highlights a broader challenge to scaling up green infrastructure on vacant lots, which is that the entities who are accountable for stormwater control and vacant land disposition can be fractured across separate agencies, making coordination and cost-sharing difficult. Other systems-level challenges for green stormwater infrastructure (and other urban greening) on vacant lots include lack of a workforce that is knowledgeable about nontraditional landscaping practices as well as technical components, such as stormwater management systems. In addition, materials are specialized. For example, native prairie plants are common to stormwater best management practices because they are low-maintenance, provide habitat, and can do well with fluctuations in soil moisture. However, native plants must be obtained from select growers, and they are limited in both quantity and seasonal availability, which makes them expensive and hard to find.

Vacant to Vibrant set out to address these systemic challenges to scaling up urban green infrastructure. Although one project cannot solve all problems for every city, our hope was that findings from our interdisciplinary team of practitioners, working through parallel planning, implementation, and maintenance processes for urban greening/vacant land use projects in three cities, could move the needle on tackling existing barriers. While the confluence of urban land vacancy, stormwater management, and neighborhood destabilization is common to many post-industrial cities, lessons learned from Vacant to Vibrant can apply to cities throughout the US that are growing their urban green space in response to demographic, economic, and climate changes. Where our lessons do not produce solutions, we hope that they provide points that advance the conversation about current barriers and inform the next iteration of innovative urban greening practices.

2

City Dynamics That Shape
Vacant Land Use

Learning the history of a neighborhood and the series of events that led to its current state sheds light on what neighborhood residents need, want, fear, hope for, know, and do not yet understand. Additionally, the way that cities have developed, and the way parts of them were demolished, have shaped the location and form of vacant land. Historical context sheds light on the physical and social attributes of vacant lots that will affect the success of urban greening projects. Urban greening projects are deeply personal features of a community that touch many residents in some way—they bring people together, build health, and build wealth. For this reason, understanding a location's history is a critical first step to developing reuse strategies for vacant lots by informing approaches to community engagement, project site selection, and design.

While it may not be practical to perform the amount of detailed historical research that is outlined in this chapter for every urban greening project, the historical context of a project can be discovered and incorporated by including residents and community partners who understand its effects implicitly, if not explicitly. Understanding this context is part of the due diligence required of a project team.

This chapter continues the story of post-industrial city decline, showing examples of research on individual neighborhoods and cities that helped inform the planning, implementation, and maintenance of Vacant to Vibrant projects. These histories illustrate how early city politics shaped citywide decision making, which today continues to be heavily influenced from the neighborhood level upward. They also show how the causes and effects of disinvestment, abandonment, and land vacancy

17

have disproportionately affected poorer residents and residents of color. Long histories of neighborhood decline and broken promises mean that trust can be difficult
to build with residents, and chief among resident concerns for new investment are
worries about how such investment will affect safety and stability in the community.
Demographic attributes provide some clues for effective approaches to community
engagement: for example, often neither older homeowners who have lived in the
neighborhood since manufacturing jobs were still good, nor younger, low-income
residents who are renting their houses, have access to a computer in the home, making in-person conversations a particularly important means of communication. Deep
connections to place and people can also help practitioners create urban greening
projects that reflect the community and avoid contributing to new risks posed by
gentrification. For urban greening and green infrastructure practitioners who are
working in a neighborhood they do not know well, finding a community liaison
who understands local history and can help bridge the gap between residents and
the project team is essential.

For stormwater management projects, neighborhood context can help mitigate
risk, pinpoint locations where projects are likely to be successful, and identify other
social and environmental problems that affect the performance of stormwater best
management practices. Past land use and demolition practices shape soil type, soil
debris, and contamination; the effects of these practices may inflate project budgets
or preclude projects altogether.

Targeting Cleveland, Gary, and Buffalo

Through a series of regional discussions during the project planning phase of Vacant
to Vibrant, the project team developed a short list of Great Lakes cities that had an
abundance of vacant land. We documented indicators that a pilot green infrastructure project would be possible and welcomed in these cities, such as the existence
of green infrastructure or urban greening pilot projects. Lastly, we were interested in
grouping cities that shared similarities that would make a common approach possible, but that had differences—such as size, geography, and potential partners—that
would yield useful lessons for people attempting similar projects in towns and cities
around the country.

Gary, Indiana; Cleveland, Ohio; and Buffalo, New York, have each lost close to 50
percent of their population over six decades. In recent years, they have undertaken a
variety of green stormwater initiatives. Gary and Buffalo benefit from having smaller
city governments with the agility required to create new systemic approaches. In addition, strong project partners in Gary and Buffalo own vacant land, which streamlined

land access and solved questions of long-term liability for maintenance. Cleveland was desirable because of its existing movements in vacant land management, which came from its early adoption of land banking, and from a consent decree–driven program to manage stormwater that was novel in its allowance for green infrastructure. Other cities considered included Milwaukee, which had an innovative sewer authority that had already shown leadership in green stormwater infrastructure. Some cities that also had a track record of green infrastructure projects, such as Grand Rapids, Michigan, were excluded because of their lack of vacant land due to their recent history of urban growth (as opposed to depopulation).

At the City of Gary, the Department of Green Urbanism had been building a case for urban revitalization through environmental stewardship. Though Gary has a reputation for being dilapidated, the city has strong potential for redevelopment given its proximity to Lake Michigan and Chicago, as well as the natural beauty of the sand dunes, beaches, and marshlands upon which it was built.

In Buffalo, People United for Sustainable Housing (PUSH) is building a workforce with expertise in turning vacant parcels into community assets to leverage other investment in energy-efficient housing, economic development, and placemaking initiatives.

In Cleveland, where the Vacant to Vibrant team leadership was based, we had neighborhood connections to community development corporations and other organizations, as well as a track record of urban greening through the Cleveland Botanical Garden's urban farming program, Green Corps.

In Vacant to Vibrant, a project team of professionals from city government, nonprofit organizations, academic institutions, and community development corporations began creating processes and plans that could be applied to urban areas in cities with vacant residential or other small parcels. Working within neighborhoods and across cities, the project team benefited from the breadth and depth of perspective on community dynamics. Although every place is unique, we were surprised by the number of lessons that transferred among neighborhoods.

Recurring Patterns

The historical context of Vacant to Vibrant neighborhoods shaped our approaches to community engagement, site selection, and project design, which were customized to fit the needs and conditions of each city. In Cleveland, data about demolition history assisted with the choice of sites that did not require costly remediation of contamination and buried debris. In all three cities, residents' concerns about urban green space were rooted in past experiences, often negative. Historical context also helped our project team understand why political processes that affected urban greening projects in our cities were shaped as much by neighborhood-level politics as by city policies—another artifact of long histories of racial and ethnic segregation.

Development of the cities of Cleveland, Gary, and Buffalo illustrates several themes that are common to many industrial cities, remnants of which persist today in neighborhood demographics, patterns of land vacancy, and decision-making processes. Each city developed around steel and manufacturing industries in the late 19th and early 20th centuries. These industries fed off a steady stream of laborers, and they reinforced social hierarchies within factories and neighborhoods. Early factory growth was aided by immigration, particularly from eastern Europe. During 1907, the year of peak European immigration, 1.2 million people flowed into the US, many of them settling in East Coast cities to work in manufacturing or to support those who did.[1] Neighborhoods were built out as families, clans, and villages from Italy, Slovakia, Hungary, Poland, Czechoslovakia, and other countries transplanted themselves into rapidly expanding industrial cities. The immigrants' ethnic identities shaped neighborhood culture and commerce.

Factories were a microcosm of city social hierarchies, where immigrants from southern and eastern European countries, most of them Catholic, were restricted mostly to blue-collar jobs. White, western European, and Protestant (and sometimes Jewish) residents occupied many executive positions, as well as positions in banking and finance. Immigrants attempted to offset the power of executives and bankers on the political stage by electing local politicians, who worked their way up into city government. Remnants of these social dynamics remain today in the way that many industrial cities continue to have decision-making processes that work from the neighborhood up, where community leaders are strong influencers in the development and implementation of city policy. (Conversely, neighborhoods that lack strong leaders or development organizations often disproportionately suffer.)

In the 1920s, when people were fleeing postwar economic downturn in Europe and the US was dealing with its own postwar recession, the federal government enacted legislation to curb immigration from many of the countries that had helped feed industrialization. The Emergency Quota Act of 1921, followed by the Immigration Act of 1924, dramatically reduced immigration from eastern and southern European countries. A US economic downturn followed until the country emerged from the Great Depression, and manufacturing demand picked up during and after World War II. In the absence of inexpensive immigrant labor from Europe, industries started recruiting heavily in the American South. Black Americans, Puerto Ricans, and Caribbeans flowed northward, filling difficult but available jobs.

When the first wave of European immigrants moved into industrial cities for jobs in steel production and manufacturing, they were given the opportunity to build neighborhoods that reflected their culture. Workers of color had fewer opportunities to do the same. Black steelworkers who started moving north in the 1930s and 1940s were heavily restricted in where they could live due to pervasive segregation practices in northern states. Black industrial laborers, their families, and others who moved north for economic opportunity were crowded into neighborhoods that were considered the least desirable to white, more affluent residents.

While desegregation in the 1950s and 1960s technically dissolved the restrictions on where black families could live, real estate agents capitalized on it to profit off the racist fears of white residents. In a process called blockbusting, real estate agents would sell one house to a black family and then stoke fears in neighboring homes that the neighborhood was on the brink of decline. This allowed real estate companies to buy homes quickly and at a discount, then sell them to black families—who were eager to have a broader choice of neighborhoods—at a premium.

White flight was swift even in the absence of such blatant profiteering, however. Except in neighborhoods where white residents staunchly protected their assets by stymieing real estate companies or by other, legal discriminatory practices, neighborhoods in urban centers in many industrial cities flipped from all-white to majority black within just a couple of decades. This demographic shift was marked by reductions in home equity, as well as withdrawal of neighborhood investment and city services.

Such patterns of demographic change and disinvestment continued through the civil rights era. Urban centers lost population to suburban areas. In midwestern and northeastern regions, employment in manufacturing alone declined by 32.9 percent between 1969 and 1996.[2] Concurrent loss of industry and population left many urban centers with a dwindling tax base, high levels of poverty and unemployment, and several thousand acres of vacant and abandoned urban land. With this vacant land came decreases in property values, visually blighted neighborhoods, and associated negative effects on crime and human health.[3]

Although the descendants of immigrants eventually dispersed, the effects of early, pervasive ethnic and racial segregation are reflected in these cities today, and not only in the cultural halls and churches that remain standing. Council members elected at the neighborhood level continue to be highly influential in the formation and enactment of city legislation.[4] Neighborhoods continue to be heavily racially segregated, and residents of color continue to endure the worst effects of neighborhood disinvestment, land vacancy, and environmental degradation.

Population loss is slowing in Cleveland, Gary, Buffalo, and cities like them.[5] In the next decade, at least one of these cities may show its first net gain since the mid-20th century. Water scarcity in western states is shining new light on the value of abundant, cheap freshwater. In preparation, Cleveland, Gary, and Buffalo are diversifying their industries, building incentives for businesses and residents, and undertaking efforts to reorient city life around their freshwater resources. At the same time, due to their manufacturing histories and position on the Great Lakes, they have been among the first targets for the US Environmental Protection Agency (USEPA) consent decrees for Clean Water Act violations. This unique confluence of pressures has forced the three cities to try to integrate green stormwater infrastructure into their blue-collar identities.

The rest of this chapter will examine the specifics of how these patterns occurred in parallel in Cleveland, Gary, and Buffalo. Similarities among these cities in cultural history and geographic attributes illustrate common needs for planning and implementation of urban greening projects on vacant lots, while differences highlight ways that Vacant to Vibrant had to be adapted to the specific needs of individual places (table 2-1).

As Vacant to Vibrant began to take shape, we familiarized ourselves with the cultural history, physical form, and ongoing initiatives within each neighborhood. Although books and written histories helped supplement our understanding, in many cases this history was shared orally, in pieces, across many conversations with diverse community members. This information guided selection of project sites and provided context for resident feedback we received over the life span of the project. While the cities are unique in many ways, themes emerged that are common to many US cities and can thus inform other communities' green infrastructure and vacant land use projects.

Cleveland: Buckeye–Woodland Hills

Sitting in a bowl carved by a glacier, Cleveland has a mostly flat natural topography. A hill on the east side of Cleveland, approximately four miles from the city center, provides one of the few natural overlooks of downtown. Before the area was developed by European settlers, this hill was known as Butternut Ridge. Later it became part of the Newburgh township, which was annexed by Cleveland in 1912 to afford space for the eastward expansion of Hungarians and Slovaks, who had displaced German and Irish immigrants in Cleveland's Lower Buckeye neighborhood. Small

Table 2-1. Characteristics of the three Vacant to Vibrant neighborhoods

Neighborhood Characteristics	Buffalo, NY West Side	Cleveland, OH Woodland Hills	Gary, IN Aetna
Population	5,395	21,059	4,671
Population (< 18) %	30	24	28
Population (18 < 65) %	64	63	61
Population (> 65) %	6	13	11
Race (black) %	22	89	82
Race (white) %	44	7	11
Race (other than black or white) %	34	4	7
Hispanic (all races) %	31	1	9
Houses with mortgage or loan %	15	24	38
Houses owned free and clear %	11	10	21
Houses rented %	74	66	41
Residents with high school diploma %	74	76	85
Median income ($)	23,003	24,151	23,519
Residents below poverty level %	40	35	37
Houses occupied %	83	74	66
Houses vacant %	17	26	34
Median home value ($)	78,433	89,238	57,900
Median monthly rent ($)	648	630	739
Tree canopy cover (%)[a,b,c]	12	24	10–20
Walkability score (city average)[d]	89 (68)	62 (60)	10 (34)

[a] American Forests, *Urban Ecosystem Analysis Buffalo-Lackawanna Area Erie County, New York* (Washington, DC: American Forests, 2003).
[b] Davey Resource Group, *The Cleveland Tree Plan* (Kent, OH: Davey Resource Group, 2015).
[c] US Forest Service, *Indiana's Forests*, Resource Bulletin NRS-45 (Washington, DC: US Forest Service, 2008).
[d] Walk Score, Redfin, http://www.walkscore.com.

factories, shops, and roads, built in proximity to railroads that stretched east, were torn down to make room for the first boulevards of Upper Buckeye. Today the entire area is known as Buckeye; within it is Woodland Hills, also called Woodhill, a small residential neighborhood on the northern side.

Cultural History

Major thoroughfares and large colonial homes, which remain today, were built starting in the late 1800s. Main streets were laid out until the 1920s, with infill housing
constructed into the next decade. The land was divided into neat parcels of approximately 40 by 100 feet, with most parcels holding a two- or three-story, one- or two-
family home with large front porches on each floor, with asphalt or cedar shake
shingles on upper floors and wood siding on the first floor.[6] Two-family homes were
a popular way for homeowners to earn extra family income by becoming a landlord,
at a time when small apartment complexes were being built across the city to address
demand for rental units.

Central European immigrants began settling the area in the 1880s. The first were
mostly Slovaks and Hungarians; the two groups were culturally distinct and somewhat hostile to each other in their home countries, but they lived, worked, and wor-
shipped side-by-side in Buckeye. Additional Hungarian immigrants arrived during
the Hungarian revolution of 1956. Black Americans began settling in larger numbers
in the 1960s and 1970s. Urban flight then began, as European descendants left for
new suburban developments.

Buckeye–Woodland Hills was home to businesses including a castings factory,
ironworks, and manufacturing facilities as well as churches, schools, and social services. Today's Woodland Hills is vastly residential. Commercial development can be
found along Buckeye Road. Rapid transit runs along Shaker Boulevard, connecting
downtown to the west, and linking Shaker Square and the suburbs to the east. Luke
Easter Park is a large, city-owned park at the southern end of the neighborhood. Luna
Park was a major destination for recreation in Cleveland until 1940, when it was
developed into a large public housing facility.

Physical Form

The natural soils in the area are loamy sands, a product of glacial till. Large amounts
of clay are commonly found in deeper soil horizons and form a barrier that is less
permeable to water and tree roots. In the mixed-hardwood forests that are native to
the region, this translates to decent drainage at the soil surface but a shallow water
table that sits atop the clay barrier. In undeveloped areas, after snow melts in the
spring but before the heat of summer, these soils form vernal pools, transient ecosystems that provide essential habitat for life-cycle stages of toads, frogs, salamanders,
microfauna, and trees. From a stormwater management perspective, during times of
heavy rain or snowmelt, water is quick to run off and overwhelm the sewer system.

A more recent soil phenomenon is the influx of clay as clean fill for development and demolition, which has significantly altered natural soils over time. In Cleveland, an important proxy for local soil conditions is the date of demolition. In the first decades of heavy demolition, it was not uncommon for contractors to simply bury building debris in the hole left by the basement. Today, the hallmark of such demolitions is a sunken depression in the shape of the building footprint, anywhere from one to three feet deep, where the debris has settled and compacted over time. Cinder block, brick, and asphalt remnants peek through the grass. Beginning in 1996, an ordinance required contractors to remove their demolition debris, which they then landfilled or, less commonly, separated and reclaimed for other products. This introduced a new trend of filling basement holes with heavy clay, which is abundant, cheap, and clean. It is then highly compacted to create the flat grade that is pleasing to local regulators and residents; these aesthetic preferences are partly in reaction to the sunken grades of past demolitions. Due to compaction, a marker of these newer demolitions is poor grass cover with high weed content in the basement footprint and poor stormwater infiltration.

In Cleveland and cities like it, where demolition rates have outpaced the speed of regulation, one never knows what is below the soil surface of vacant parcels; one might plant a shovel and find a block of heavy clay, a bad scenario for stormwater management. Alternatively, on one vacant lot that was put into stormwater management as part of a separate project, we discovered a century-old brick patio that covered one-third of the parcel eight inches below the surface.

While debris can create pore space that infiltrates water, it complicates soil preparation and can dramatically inflate excavation and disposal costs. Undocumented underground gas or oil storage tanks are also very common and, unfortunately, are likely to be found on nearly any corner lot in a neighborhood that has been historically zoned for mixed use.

Neighborhood Context

On a map depicting the northwest corner of the neighborhood, five quiet residential streets run parallel within a square between two main thoroughfares to downtown (figure 2-1). On their total length of nearly one-half mile, there are no cross streets; an overgrown, unmaintained walking path provides the only connection between blocks for the few residents who use it.

Woodland Hills benefits from the presence of a number of strong community nonprofit and philanthropic organizations that are engaged in economic development and placemaking in this neighborhood. Just north of the project site is Holden Forests & Gardens'[7] largest Green Corps urban farm, which was the community

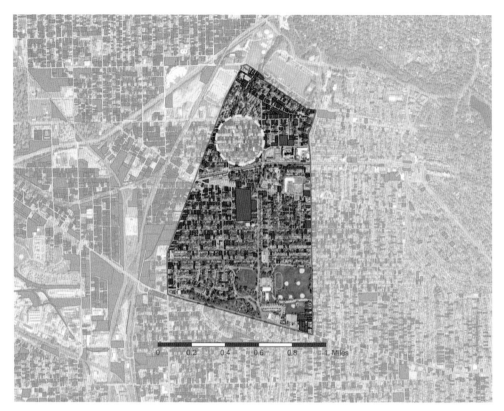

Figure 2-1. Vacant to Vibrant project sites (black) and untreated sites for comparison (white) in the Woodland Hills neighborhood of Cleveland. Other vacant parcels shaded in gray. Data sources: NEOCANDO and City of Cleveland, Esri.

partner originally set to be responsible for site maintenance for Vacant to Vibrant projects (this plan changed later, as explained in chapter 5).

Vacant to Vibrant drew inspiration from a larger conversation within Cleveland about ways to repurpose vacant parcels for community benefit. Sparked by the city's 20,000 vacant parcels, in 2008, city government and local nonprofit agencies started the Re-Imagining Cleveland initiative to pilot a series of grassroots vacant lot reuse projects scattered across the city. Over several years, the initiative led to the creation of 156 projects, including community and market gardens, pocket parks, a vineyard, stormwater management features, and side-yard projects.[8] Building on Re-Imagining Cleveland, the Cleveland City Planning Commission convened a series of eight interdisciplinary working groups to create recommendations for sustainable use projects on vacant lots; one working group was dedicated to stormwater management.[9]

The Vacant to Vibrant projects are located approximately one mile south of a

(box 2-1)

Box 2-1. Cleveland historical context

In Cleveland, the project team benefited from having access to detailed data about demolition, which were incorporated into the process of choosing project sites to reduce the risk of finding contamination or debris that would warrant costly removal. Planning also took into consideration the presence of local green infrastructure and urban greening initiatives.

large green infrastructure site, designed to capture 17 million gallons of stormwater per year from sewer separation of nearby properties (box 2-1). The project belongs to the Northeast Ohio Regional Sewer District (NEORSD), serving the greater Cleveland area. In 2011, NEORSD entered into a consent decree with USEPA and Ohio EPA[10] due to discharges of untreated sewage from its combined sewer system, a violation of the Clean Water Act.[11] At the time of the consent decree, NEORSD was discharging 4.5 billion gallons of untreated water annually through 126 permitted outfall locations, in violation of its NPDES permits. Its program to bring its system back into compliance by reducing discharges to approximately 500 million gallons annually (translating to 98 percent capture), dubbed "Project Clean Lake," includes a mixture of deep storage tunnels and other large storage devices, as well as upgrades to pump stations and water treatment facilities. Of note, the long-term control plan also contains an allowance for green infrastructure—the first consent decree to allow this—to mitigate at least 44 million gallons of combined sewer overflow via green infrastructure. The estimated cost of remedying the problem will be $3 billion over 25 years, although NEORSD reported in 2018 that it expected actual costs to ratepayers to be significantly less than originally projected due to a number of cost-saving measures.

Gary: Aetna

The Aetna neighborhood in eastern Gary, Indiana, sits between the city's industrial corridor to the west and the beachfront neighborhood of Miller to the east. Aetna predates Gary; it was established in 1881 as a company town of mostly male residents for a munitions manufacturer, the Aetna Powder Company. Its remote location in northwest Indiana, among dunes and marshes, was well suited to the explosive nature of its product, used to uproot tree stumps and boulders for farming. (Several detonations and explosions had led residents from surrounding towns to regard the plant as a nuisance.) From the beginning, Aetna and Gary would be shaped by the booms, busts, environmental effects, and racial tensions that came with being a company town.

Cultural History

The nearby city of Gary was founded in 1906, when US Steel built the Gary Works plant—the largest steel mill in the world for many years, and today the largest integrated steel mill in North America—in proximity to Chicago and the Great Lakes. Its residents were diverse; in 1920, 60 percent of residents of Gary were foreign-born or first-generation Americans, mostly of Eastern European descent. Another 18 percent were black. Social hierarchy around the steel plant and in the city was based on class and race, which dictated where people worked, lived, and played, as well as their level of exposure to pollutants in air and water. When federal policies restricted immigration from Eastern European countries in the mid-1920s, black and Mexican workers were recruited from the American South to fill jobs at Gary Works. Most of the jobs available to these southern newcomers came with low pay, low status, and the highest exposure to risk and pollution of all the work at the plant.

The City of Gary officially annexed Aetna and nearby Miller in 1928 to help alleviate a housing shortage. Black steelworkers were restricted to homes in the densely packed Midtown district, so early suburban growth was fed mostly by relocation of white residents. Many of these were children of Eastern European immigrants who were looking to leave the cramped downtown area for private homes in cleaner neighborhoods (although air quality in the suburbs did not end up being as good as advertised). While both the Aetna and Miller neighborhoods benefited from white flight, beachfront property attracted more affluent families to Miller. Its residents then successfully organized themselves around efforts that would keep the neighborhood predominantly white and affluent, although it could not fully escape the water and air quality issues from Gary Works. Still, it remained somewhat insulated from the serious economic downturn that later affected other parts of Gary. For this reason, Miller continues to serve as an important reference point for Aetna and the rest of Gary, one with dramatically different incomes, property values, and access to quality green space than the rest of the city.

By the 1940s, the Gary Works plant was operating at full capacity to fulfill the demands of both World War II and record automobile sales. For the next two decades, Gary boomed and Aetna grew into a lively community, its expansion aided by new freeways that increased access to downtown from the suburbs. The suburbs officially opened to black residents during the 1950s, but it was not until two decades later that Gary saw the dramatic demographic shift that persists to the present day.

By 1969, black steelworkers in Gary had a higher median income than in any other US city, though it was still lower than that of the city's white steelworkers. Following the election of the first black mayor in 1967, realtors capitalized on racial fears to convert entire neighborhoods from white to black via blockbusting. Public and private neighborhood investment, as well as city services such as trash pickup, slowed or stopped as neighborhoods acquired more black residents. Many neighborhoods flipped from majority white to majority black in the 1970s and 1980s, and residents lost the opportunity afforded to former white residents to build wealth via their investment in housing (box 2-2).[12]

Unlike other post-industrial cities, Gary saw steel production continue well into the 1980s, illustrating that the "Rust Belt" phenomenon was not directly linked to deindustrialization. The city was doing poorly by that time, however. Over its history, US Steel had exploited social and racial tensions to avoid environmental responsibility for the contamination it caused to land, water, and air.

Environmental activism had sprung up to combat the increasingly poor air quality, disease, and impaired recreation at work and at home, but there were disagreements between white and black steelworkers, as well as between poorer and more affluent residents, about which environmental concerns should take priority. Environmental movements driven by black and poorer residents in Gary tended to organize around access to necessary resources and safe living conditions, while environmental movements driven by white and more affluent residents often focused on preserving recreation amenities that they were far more likely than other residents to use. Such tensions among stakeholder groups reduced the power of the steelworkers' union and spilled into the rest of the community. During the 1970s progress was made toward environmental cleanup, but in the 1980s conservative politics at the federal and other levels of government undid much of it.[13]

Physical Form

The soil in the western end of Aetna, on the southern shore of Lake Michigan, is 95 percent sand or more, looking much like the dunes that surround the neighborhood to the west and south. These soils infiltrate water quickly, but the shallow water table beneath most of the neighborhood leaves water with little place to go. During heavy rains and snowmelt, the water table rises quickly, flooding streets and basements from below in places.

Many houses in the Aetna neighborhood are vacant. Some have been empty for so long—15 years or more—that neighbors do not remember who used to live there. In recent years, Hardest Hit dollars have allowed the city to make inroads on demolition of such abandoned houses. Demolition is urgent not only to stabilize housing values in the rest of the neighborhood but also to curb a pernicious problem caused by contractors and waste haulers from Chicagoland, who have long used Aetna and

Gary as a dumping ground for waste materials. They pack houses and vacant lots with debris to save themselves the cost and hassle of disposal, creating fire hazards for local residents and necessitating costly contamination remediation by demolition contractors.

Neighborhood Context

Today's Aetna neighborhood is composed mostly of modest colonial- and bungalow-style residential houses. There are a few small and large park spaces (many of them in advanced stages of disrepair), a few local churches, and the building that housed Aetna Elementary School, which closed in 2005. Gary currently has 80,000 residents;

Figure 2-2. Vacant to Vibrant project sites (black) and untreated sites for comparison (white) in the Aetna neighborhood of Gary. Other vacant parcels shaded in gray. Data sources: City of Gary, Esri.

it is at approximately 45 percent of its peak size in 1960 and still shrinking. Because of isolation created by highways, the structure of its streets, and the low density of its commercial development, residents of Aetna are reliant on cars to get to work, recreation, grocery stores, and amenities (figure 2-2).

The City of Gary's Department of Environmental Affairs and Green Urbanism has built a portfolio of green stormwater management to catalyze community resiliency. They have successfully garnered projects and leveraged funds for demolition of houses and a prominent Sheraton hotel that had become an iconic vacant eyesore; for vacant land reuse (including Vacant to Vibrant) and stormwater infrastructure that helped rebuild green streets; and for protection of dunes, marshland, and beachfront as community and environmental assests.

Several separate, integrated community planning processes have led to green infrastructure as a prominent feature of lakefront and neighborhood plans. City work agreements incorporate requirements to work with Gary-based contractors and goods and, when possible, to incorporate the city's nascent urban green space workforce, the Urban Conservation Team, to help ensure that funds have maximum benefit to the local economy. This focus recognizes and works to correct the long-standing exclusion of black residents from the rewards of local economic development.

In 2016 Gary Sanitary District and the City of Gary entered into a consent decree with USEPA and the state's Department of Environmental Management to address wastewater and stormwater discharges, an update to several agreements that had been enacted between 1979 and 2003.[14] The 2016 consent decree outlined plans to curb combined sewer overflows and perform ecological restoration along riparian areas in northwest Indiana, including on the Grand Calumet River. To reduce financial burdens on ratepayers for activities related to the consent decree, and to provide relief for other long-standing environmental problems, the city has been aggressive in pursuing green infrastructure grants to alleviate stormwater runoff and create green amenities for residents. The 2008 Gary Comprehensive Plan notes that the city lacks sufficient park space and calls for vacant lots to be preserved as an opportunity

Box 2-2. Gary historical context

The historical context that shaped Vacant to Vibrant project implementation in Gary included long-standing segregation and exploitation of non-white residents, which translated into a strong community desire to capture economic investment for the benefit of Gary residents. For this reason, city government and residents placed special emphasis on sourcing materials and labor from within city limits, to the extent possible.

for neighborhood development, stormwater collection, public green space, and an interconnected trail system. Green infrastructure planning ramped up in 2013 with the receipt of a Technical Assistance Grant from USEPA to engage the community to design green stormwater infrastructure. An update to the Gary Comprehensive Plan, begun in 2018, will intensify the city's focus on green infrastructure planning and economic development.[15]

Buffalo: West Side

Main Street divides the city of Buffalo, New York, into the East Side and West Side. The West Side neighborhood sits just north of downtown Buffalo, along the Niagara River. People United for Sustainable Housing (PUSH), a community-based organization that started on Buffalo's West Side in 2005, has helped orchestrate resident-led public campaigns to address the lack of jobs as well as neighborhood conditions when they were in rapid decline, with widespread housing abandonment. Their work encompasses affordable housing, sustainability, green infrastructure, and green job creation and training. PUSH-facilitated community efforts within their footprint have led to vastly more housing stock with rents that are fair and reasonable to residents regardless of income.

Cultural History

White settlers began displacing Seneca peoples from the Buffalo region in the early 1800s, and by 1850 Buffalo had become a significant steel and manufacturing city due to its connections to the Erie Canal and the Great Lakes. By the late 19th century, the West Side was booming with immigrant laborers, particularly Italians and Eastern Europeans, who were predominantly Catholic.[16] Several generations of one family often lived near each other in the same neighborhood and worked in the same industry.

Then, in the 1920s, federal restrictions on immigration from the countries whose people had helped build early Buffalo's neighborhoods were enacted. An influx of black residents from the American South, many from rural areas, as well as Puerto Rican and other Caribbean immigrants, arrived to keep factories running. As in other cities, black residents were subject to restrictions on where they could live, preventing racial integration of the neighborhoods.

Ethnic and racial identities shaped the character of Buffalo's neighborhoods but also blurred the lines between community and politics. Residents of working-class neighborhoods lived mostly separate lives from the business establishment and economic elite, so their access to power lay in politics, where careers began at the neighborhood level. With a large Democratic majority and few Republican politicians in the fray, many civic decisions were racially or ethnically motivated (box 2-3).[17]

In the late 1800s, the Italian, Hungarian, Polish, and German neighborhoods were so self-contained that proposals to create a central downtown business district were considered superfluous. Streetcars and American-born children soon changed that, however. Construction of streetcars near the turn of the 20th century connected ethnic neighborhoods to downtown Buffalo. This new mobility drained neighborhood business districts and diluted cultural monocultures. By the 1920s, automobiles had bled business from downtown too, by making it easier for downtown workers to efficiently shuttle from the workplace back to their neighborhood business districts.

The opening of the St. Lawrence Seaway in 1959 created a direct route between the Great Lakes and the Atlantic Ocean. This severely hampered the commercial economy in Buffalo and increased reliance on industry, leaving the city's economy vulnerable to the decline in domestically produced steel and automobiles that was to come.[18]

Environmental degradation took place in parallel with industrialization. The Buffalo and Niagara Rivers were used to dispose of industrial waste for many years, especially in the 1940s.[19] In 1949, the US Public Health Service declared the Niagara River to be one of "the most seriously polluted rivers in the United States." Both the Buffalo and Niagara Rivers were designated as separate Areas of Concern under the 1987 Great Lakes Water Quality Agreement due to industrial and municipal (including sewer) discharges that contaminated water and sediment and killed wildlife in the rivers and in Lake Erie. Swimming and fishing are not officially allowed, although they take place anyway and are particularly popular among immigrant residents.

Physical Form

The soil in the area has proven challenging for stormwater management. Composed of intertwining fingers of sand and clay, it can compact into a dense brick that is very difficult to manipulate and can generate a lot of runoff. The focus of stormwater management on the West Side includes promoting plant growth for evapotranspiration[20] and to break up the soil, slowing sheet flow across the surface, and building the water-holding capacity of the soil with organic material.

PUSH's green infrastructure is now part of larger efforts within the city of Buffalo to make use of vacant lots and clean the city's water. In 2014, USEPA and the New York State Department of Environmental Conservation approved a long-term management plan from the City of Buffalo and the Buffalo Sewer Authority to reduce sewer and stormwater runoff flowing into local waterways via the combined sewer system.[21] The long-term control plan follows a 2012 compliance order from USEPA and commits the Buffalo Sewer Authority to reducing 1.75 billion gallons of untreated discharges over 20 years, at a cost of around $380 million. Investments include $93 million on green stormwater infrastructure to remove between 1,315 and 1,620 acres of impervious surface through vacant lot modifications and demolition. The long-term control plan also aims for a goal of 60 percent downspout disconnection and 60 percent green streets.

Neighborhood Context

As part of their urban greening work, PUSH has installed and maintained community gardens and green infrastructure sites to create a Green Development Zone, a 25-block area with vacant lots that have been converted into a variety of urban greening projects that serve the community (figure 2-3). The Green Development Zone features 120 parcels that incorporate renewable energy, green housing rehabilitation, urban farming, and green stormwater infrastructure. In total, it is estimated that these projects—and the ongoing PUSH programs that support them—have created 100 living-wage jobs, reduced carbon emissions by 155 metric tons per year, and created 90 units of affordable sustainable housing.[22]

Buffalo's West Side differs from Woodland Hills and Aetna in its high level of mixed residential and commercial land uses. The neighborhood is dotted with shops, restaurants, and cafes that serve local and world cuisine, with a main strip of commercial development on Grant Street. Recent decades have seen an increase in immigrants from Somalia, Sudan, and Burma, creating a diverse neighborhood where over 40 languages are spoken. Mixed-use development of moderate density, plus connections to major thoroughfares, give the area a footprint that is very walkable, with good transit and good bike access.

The city adopted an updated city plan in 2017, the Buffalo Green Code, which promotes sustainable land use by incorporating regulations for stormwater capture, tree preservation, green landscaping, and waterfront revitalization. The code further allows for land

Box 2-3. Buffalo historical context

Political history shaped the community decision-making processes in Buffalo, resulting in strong neighborhood influence on policy development and implementation. The work of PUSH Buffalo illustrates what is possible with a strong community partner; their involvement greatly aided the success of Vacant to Vibrant there.

Figure 2-3. Vacant to Vibrant project sites (black) and untreated sites for comparison (white) in the West Side neighborhood of Buffalo. Other vacant parcels shaded in gray. Data sources: City of Buffalo, Esri.

banking and outlines interim and permanent uses for vacant parcels. In a separate vacant land initiative, student researchers at the University at Buffalo (led by Vacant to Vibrant project team member Sean Burkholder) quantified stormwater capture on thousands of vacant lots.[23] Their dataset has contributed to vacant parcels and demolition being counted as green infrastructure under the Buffalo Sewer Authority's long-term control plan.

Comparing the Three Cities

These three neighborhoods in three cities, chosen for their similarities and their interest in utilizing vacant lots for green infrastructure, provide a useful comparison of the systems and processes that contribute to the success of an urban greening initiative. Buckeye–Woodland Hills in Cleveland, Aetna in Gary, and Buffalo's West Side are similar in their development around steel and manufacturing, as well as in their climate, residential demographics, regulatory mandates, and position on the Great Lakes. How would such similarities affect land access, project implementation, resident engagement, and maintenance within cities of different sizes, with different politics, partnering organizations, and local regulatory frameworks?

Understanding the histories of each neighborhood—how its land came to be developed and, over time, demolished—sheds light on the physical and social dynamics of neighborhoods that affect urban greening projects. This historical context then informed project planning, as described in the next chapter, which specifically examines how the project team chose project sites, how they listened to residents' concerns and created methods for engagement, and, finally, how they designed projects to capture stormwater runoff and help stabilize neighborhoods.

3

Vacant to Vibrant Planning

One objective of the Vacant to Vibrant project was to test whether disparate land uses—neighborhood recreation and stormwater management—could coexist within the small confines of a vacant parcel. Not only does combining land uses make efficient use of space, but we believe that it may protect urban green space from future development by expanding the group of stakeholders who are invested in its preservation.

A potential downside to combining land uses, however, is the risk that they will interfere with each other in the social and/or environmental benefits they provide. For example, running or playing in rain gardens can compact soil and impede infiltration, while standing water within recreation areas interferes with enjoyment of play equipment, paths, and benches. In early phases of the project, when we were unsure how much space would be required for stormwater management, these risks seemed more uncertain. As the project progressed, we found that we could reduce the footprint of rain gardens at the surface by increasing belowground storage, and that sites with a gentle slope could direct stormwater flow away from recreation features, reducing interference. Additionally, some land uses, such as more passive recreation provided by birdhouses and flower beds, were less likely to conflict with stormwater capture.

Planning and community engagement were both aided by a broader understanding of historical context, which was outlined in previous chapters. This context shed light on how several decades of urban decline had made some residents nervous about how new investment in the neighborhood would affect their safety and inclusion. Knowledge of past land use, demolition history, and current neighbor-hood conditions was important to understand physical attributes, such as soil com-paction, contamination, and dumping, that could affect project installation. This chapter describes the application of neighborhood research, community engage-ment, and design to project planning.

Selecting Vacant Parcels for Urban Greening Use

While project location and the physical characteristics of sites have a large impact on project success, in common practice urban greening sites are often selected for rea-sons unrelated to performance. Even with hundreds or thousands of vacant parcels, it is common for urban greening sites to be chosen using a bottom-up (parcel-level), rather than a top-down, process. A site may be chosen because of location, or because it is accessible, or because it is an eyesore; then a project is designed to fit that site. For example, soil or topographic characteristics that affect the flow or infiltration of runoff are often not considered until late in the planning process. In other cases, it is common for innovative urban greening projects to be placed within wealthier communities, due to a perception that such locations will increase the visibility of a project, so that urban greening's potential to help build equity in underserved neigh-borhoods is often not realized.[1]

For cost efficiency, and to maximize the functionality of green stormwater infra-structure on a larger scale, such as at the level of the watershed or region, a top-down approach to selecting sites should be more frequently used. Few resources provide guid-ance for such an approach to urban greening, however. With this in mind, the Vacant to Vibrant team tested a process that could be useful for projects with the flexibility to take a top-down approach to siting projects. Using an array of site characteristics and criteria that we deemed important for project success, we whittled a long list of vacant parcels down to a cluster of three, located within a short distance of one another, in each city. Where possible, we used publicly available data sets and open-source GIS software to help automate decision making to make the process replicable for other projects. A drawback to this method is that it requires specialized knowledge of GIS software and data processing, but a benefit is that it increases the chances that projects will function as intended. It may also lower risk and its associated costs by avoiding sources of contamination and reducing the amount of excavation and grading that is required, both of which can quickly consume a modest project budget.

From this process, we developed a list of project goals that operated at different spatial scales and created a method for selecting sites that worked at three progres-sively smaller spatial extents (figure 3-1).

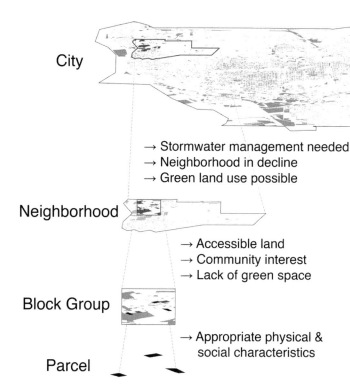

City

→ Stormwater management needed
→ Neighborhood in decline
→ Green land use possible

Neighborhood

→ Accessible land
→ Community interest
→ Lack of green space

Block Group

→ Appropriate physical &
   social characteristics

Parcel

Figure 3-1. Vacant to Vibrant tested a top-down process for selecting vacant parcels for stormwater parks, applying criteria for site selection at the level of the city, down through progressively smaller spatial extents. Data source: City of Buffalo.

City

In Cleveland, the process of selecting Vacant to Vibrant sites started at the level of the city, which, in 2012, had grown to more than 25,000 vacant parcels. (In Gary and Buffalo, neighborhoods were identified first by our community partners, and then vacant parcels within those neighborhoods were evaluated and narrowed down to project sites.) To narrow down neighborhoods to those where green infrastructure would be both appropriate and successful, at the level of the city we considered neighborhood stabilization target areas, stormwater management priority areas, and places where urban greening was a permissible land use (table 3-1). We prioritized neighborhoods that had received investment of federal, state, and/or local dollars for economic stabilization or redevelopment; neighborhoods where stormwater management was a priority, whether due to flooding or combined sewer overflow (CSO); and neighborhoods that had active urban farming, land reuse programs, or a formal green zoning designation.

To start to address problems of environmental inequality, we also considered the demographic composition of each community, prioritizing underserved neighborhoods with large racial or ethnic minority populations and below-median income.

When our project started, there was not much overlap between green stormwater management and vacant land reuse, in terms of either people or processes. Even today, a separation exists between urban farming movements, which have roots in political movements to mitigate food scarcity, environmental injustice, and neighborhood disinvestment, and green stormwater infrastructure movements, which are primarily driven by environmental considerations. These differences recall divisions (described in chapter 2) between poorer steelworkers, who had less access to safe, healthy homes, food, and water, and more affluent steelworkers, who organized around preserving the quality of their recreational spaces. A lesson from urban farming is that ecologically minded projects can improve social conditions of neighborhoods; the chances of this are higher when social factors are considered at the time of siting and designing projects.

At the level of the city, we also considered whether we could gain access to vacant parcels, taking into consideration zoning restrictions, land banking, and permission to access land via agreements or by partnering directly with landowners. We used these factors to prioritize neighborhoods where there was a structure in place to access land, such as through agreements with owners who were amenable to green reuse and other project priorities.

Neighborhood

To build upon the work of other initiatives, we considered existing or potential community partners within each neighborhood. Northside Redevelopment and the federal Hardest Hit programs in Gary were important municipal projects with goals parallel to those of Vacant to Vibrant. Alignment with existing organizations—People United for Sustainable Housing (PUSH) and Buckeye Shaker Square Development Corporation—influenced our selections in Buffalo and Cleveland. At the neighborhood level, we also laid the groundwork for considerations that would be fleshed out at finer scales, taking into account the density of existing parks and green space; density of vacant land; socioeconomic attributes; access via public transit, walking, and biking; and whether stormwater management priorities had been designated by local sewer authorities.

Block group

Once a neighborhood was chosen, we used environmental and socioeconomic data from the US Geological Survey and US Census Bureau to narrow down block groups of interest, the smallest geographical unit for which census data were available (table 3-2). Environmental considerations included the following:

Table 3-1. Selection criteria for Vacant to Vibrant candidate neighborhoods

Criteria	Possible Indicators	Example Metrics
Stormwater management target area	Sewer district target area Green zoning designation Lack of compliance with state or federal laws that govern stormwater or combined sewer discharges	CSO events/gallons per year Gallons of untreated water released Existing green infrastructure Required compliance metrics
Neighborhood stabilization target area	Federal, state investment for stabilization or demolition City planning designation Existing moderate levels, or growing rates, of vacancy/abandonment	Institutional density (schools, assisted living facilities, libraries, rec centers) Population density and rate of change Demographic information Demolition rate House occupancy
Urban greening permitted	Farming/gardening presence Existing/planned urban greening projects Formal designation as area that permits/encourages green infrastructure Green reuse welcomed by residents	Urban farms and community gardens Private gardens Green stormwater control measures

- *Sewersheds with high volumes of CSO:* Green stormwater infrastructure would be more effective at impacting water quality in these areas (such information was available for Cleveland).
- *Parcel location within the watershed:* Locations higher in the watershed were prioritized, on the assumption that distributed green infrastructure may be more effective here by collecting runoff before it can enter the sewer system.
- *Proximity of parcels to existing green space:* We looked for parcels that were farther from green amenities, to prioritize neighborhoods that did not already have parks.
- *Slope and contour of the area:* Flatter and more even parcels were prioritized on the assumption that they would require less grading and would not slope into street drains.

Social and economic data from the 2010 US Census[2] factored in block-group and census-tract levels of income, racial makeup, ages, and home values. Census and field survey–based vacancy rates provided an assessment of the need for neighborhood stabilization, which allowed us to look for areas that had a variety of vacant parcels to select from, as well as resident density that would ensure substantial public benefit from a new amenity. Proximity to other community enhancement programs was also an important selection factor, because we were looking to build on momentum from other types of local investment; during this phase we relied on extensive consultation with neighborhood partners.

Parcel

Once we had a neighborhood of focus, we used a combination of quantitative and qualitative analyses to narrow candidate parcels to a list of three that could be converted to stormwater parks (table 3-3). In addition, we identified three similar nearby parcels that would remain vacant for the purposes of comparison for ecological monitoring (described in chapter 6). We analyzed GIS parcel information and census data to identify vacant parcels that were owned by city government or a collaborating institution, and that we would be able to work on via a lease or other type of agreement. Using terrain maps from the US Geological Survey that had been derived from remotely sensed data (approximately

Table 3-2. Selection criteria for Vacant to Vibrant candidate census block groups

Criteria	Possible Indicators	Example Metrics
Land can be accessed	Publicly owned vacant lots	Vacant parcels/vacant land area
	Private vacant lots with owner who supports green reuse	Existing lease agreements
		Side yards
	Public vacant land lease/purchase programs	
Existing land infiltrates stormwater	Soils infiltrate water	Clay content
	Water table sufficiently low	Infiltration rates
	Local topography appropriate for collecting stormwater	Water table depth
		Topography: slope, slope variability
	Majority of demolition occurred ca. 1996 or later (i.e., lower likelihood of demo debris)	Impervious surface area
		Frequent flooded areas
Area located within single sewershed	No abrupt changes in large topographical features	Topography: elevation, slope
		Sewer/watershed location
	Sewer maps suggest same sewershed	

11-foot resolution), we examined the topography within a 100-foot buffer area around each parcel to identify land features such as steepness, compass direction of the main slope(s), and whether the land was roughly convex or concave—properties that could influence how easily stormwater could be captured and held on site (table 3-4a).

One exception was Buffalo, where high-resolution maps were not available; fortunately, Buffalo's parcels tended to be uniformly flat, and terrain differences were not large enough to warrant separation based on topography. Here, our project partner PUSH had identified candidate parcels that they owned (as Buffalo Neighborhood Stabilization Corporation) and had approved for use as stormwater management.

Once the list of possible sites was narrowed down to a manageable number, we used Google Maps and field reconnaissance to evaluate parcels on 12 qualitative, binary (yes/no) criteria (table 3-4b). In some cases, qualitative criteria were created to confirm or

Table 3-2. Continued

Criteria	Possible Indicators	Example Metrics
Moderate land vacancy	Aerial photography, parcel-level data sets, and/or site visits show vacancy	Vacant parcels/vacant land area
		Vacant parcel average size, density, connectivity
		Demolition history
Moderate house occupancy	60% or more of houses are occupied	Home occupancy
		Rental rates
		Population density
		Postal vacancy rates
Demand for recreation	Neighborhood violent crime rates not so high as to discourage recreation	Crime rates
		Institutional density
	Foot/bike traffic	Existing recreational space
	Located close to school, assisted living facility, public transport	Resident feedback
		Residents living with 10-minute walk of park
	Sufficient demand for (more) recreational space	Foot paths, tire swings
	Signs of informal recreational use	
Urban greening welcomed	Neighborhood plans incorporate urban greening	Parcels in green reuse
		Green zoning designations
	Urban green space is a desired potential land use	Resident feedback
	Existing green reuse	

Table 3-3. Selection criteria for Vacant to Vibrant candidate vacant parcels

Criteria	Possible Indicators	Example Metrics
Parcel appropriate for passive–active use	Nearby residences, businesses, schools Low near-term redevelopment potential Low conservation need	Institutional density Nearby occupancy Indicators of informal recreation use
Soils will permit stormwater infiltration	No seasonal/episodic standing water Low clay content Low compaction Topography appropriate for collecting stormwater	Bulk density Infiltration rate Soil core inspection Slope
Parcels do not pose contamination hazard	Not brownfields Past/present land use does not raise concerns for contamination (no underground tanks, tire/chemical dumps, dry cleaners)	Site history: public records, oral history Soil testing: contaminants
Excavation likely to be uncomplicated	Known land use & demolition history Demolition occurred under ordinances governing removal of demo debris Not a known past dumping ground	Site history Soil core inspection
Current land use in line with recreational use	Currently used as a cut-through, playing field, or gathering place Not adjacent to parcels or features that pose a safety hazard Residents are on board	Site visit Indicators of current use Resident feedback
Parcel access can be secured	Ordinances permit urban greening Purchase, lease, or other agreement possible	Ownership Zoning Property value

supplement quantitative data that had been remotely sensed. Criteria were weighted to give priority to attributes that were more important to the project team, and each parcel was assigned a score based on these weighted criteria. We then ranked candidate vacant parcels based on qualitative and quantitative criteria. Using these metrics to screen candidate parcels produced a ranked list of parcels that were most suitable for green infrastructure. These parcels were then paired using the statistical method of principal component analysis, which identifies how similar parcels are to one another based on multiple criteria. Pairs were divided into treated parcels that were to be built into green

Table 3-4a. Quantitative criteria used to evaluate parcel suitability for recreation and stormwater management

Quantitative Criteria	Explanation
Occupied houses within 100 feet of parcel (number)	Indicates localized housing occupancy. Are there enough residents nearby to benefit from a project?
Curvature of parcel (sum)	How concave or convex a parcel is. It is easier to collect stormwater runoff on concave parcels.
Curvature of area within 100 feet of parcel (sum)	How concave/convex area around parcel is. Parcels that sit within a localized depression can collect runoff from adjacent parcels.
Slope of parcel (mean)	Steepness of slope, averaged across parcel. Parcels with a steep slope are harder to use for recreation.
Slope of parcel (standard deviation)	Variability of slope. Can indicate depressions where older demolition debris collapsed into basement, or hills of soil/debris that would require regrading/removal.
Slope of area within 100 feet of parcel (mean)	Steepness, averaged across surrounding area. Hills obstruct views onto parcel; parcels within depressions can collect runoff from adjacent parcels.
Aspect of parcel in compass degrees (mean)	Compass direction of hills and depressions on parcel give information about direction of runoff flow.
Aspect of parcel in compass degrees of area within 100 feet (mean)	Compass direction of hills and depressions surrounding parcel give information about direction of runoff flow.

infrastructure and untreated parcels that would remain undeveloped for comparison.

Among the parcel selection criteria that we considered for stormwater management and recreation, we found that the density of nearby occupied houses and the relative flatness of parcels were particularly helpful in narrowing down parcels to sites that would be suitable for mixed recreation and stormwater management. Nearby occupied houses helped us identify lots that were located among neighbors who could use and benefit from them. How flat a parcel was (how little its slope varied) helped us identify the potential for holding stormwater on site.

From these analyses, we recommended 15 candidate parcels to our Cleveland community partners for closer examination. In Gary, we had the added ability to consider parcels that contained empty houses, which could be demolished using Hardest Hit funds. An advantage of working in collaboration with the city's demolition

Table 3-4b. Qualitative criteria used to evaluate parcel suitability for recreation and stormwater management

Qualitative Criteria (Y/N)	Explanation
Area around the parcel does not present obvious concerns for safety/stability	Obvious problems on adjacent parcels such as guard dogs, drug activity, or safety concerns excluded parcels from consideration. (weight = 1)
Parcel grade is not significantly different from sidewalk grade	On some streets, houses were built on hills that were positioned above street level; runoff from these parcels flows into streets. (weight = 1)
No high-quality trees on site	Valuable trees would need to be incorporated into project design; trees of poor quality would need to be removed. (weight = 1)
Parcel slopes away from street	Parcels that slope from street could naturally divert street flow. (weight = 1)
No hills or depressions that might indicate buried debris	Housing debris or dumping on site would require remediation before construction. (weight = 1)
Curb at the street is absent	Parcels without street curbs could naturally collect street flow. (weight = 0.1 [less important])
Sidewalk is intact and level	Parcels without sidewalks, or with very uneven sidewalks, would require construction, a significant community benefit but also cost. (weight = 0.1)
Driveway apron has been removed	Historical driveways and aprons make it easier to drive onto the parcel, encouraging parking and dumping on site. (weight = 0.1)
Fire hydrant present	A fire hydrant is a potential water source. (weight = 0.1)
No adjacent street drain	Street drains divert flow from stormwater management features into combined sewer systems. (weight = 0.1)
Parcel is not an existing side yard	Many cities sell vacant lots to adjacent homeowners at a discount, for ongoing maintenance ("side yard"). Side yards are not publicly accessible. (weight = 0.1)
Signs of existing informal use	Parcels that are already used as cut-throughs, play lots, or gathering spots indicate demand for more formal programming. (weight = 0.1)

program was the ability to coordinate with the demolition contractor on post-demo-lition grading and filling, which could be done to project specifications, saving costs of extensive grading and ensuring that fill had good drainage properties.

The project team worked collectively to select the final set of parcels. In Cleveland, the pool of 15 candidate parcels was narrowed down with parcel information from county databases. Demolition practices and history were important determinants—we used this information to minimize risk of contamination remediation, to keep project budgets small. For example, we avoided parcels with older demolitions (prior to 1996 in Cleveland), when it was customary to bury demolition debris on site in the histori-cal basement footprint. We also avoided parcels where demolition had taken place dur-ing years when heavy clay fill was more commonly used, where it would be more dif-ficult to infiltrate water into deeper soil layers. In Gary, the Hardest Hit program moved along concurrently with our selection process. Two post-demolition parcels and one vacant city-owned parcel were selected as our three experimental sites. The remaining untreated sites that would be monitored in parallel as reference points were selected based on their availability and similarity to treatment parcels.

Parcel Suitability Summary

We combined multiple data sources to pilot an automated process for top-down par-cel selection for Vacant to Vibrant project sites based on criteria that made project success more likely and minimized risk. Lessons from this process can be applied to evaluating sites for a variety of vacant land reuse and urban greening projects. Draw-ing heavily from publicly available data sets in the interest of transferability to other types of land uses, we tested the ability to quickly whittle down large numbers of candidate parcels using remotely sensed data. In this way, we eliminated hundreds of parcels where it would be more difficult to collect stormwater runoff, or where recre-ation amenities would be less useful to the neighborhood. The resultant, smaller set of candidate parcels could then be investigated using more time-intensive methods, such as site visits and community interviews.

The criteria for parcel suitability that we chose do not form an exhaustive list for all urban greening projects, but they are an example of the types of readily available information that can identify ease of collecting stormwater runoff or point to poten-tial problem areas. Project leaders can finalize their parcel suitability criteria based on their own project objectives and information that is available to them. The Vacant to Vibrant project team benefited heavily from volunteer expertise donated by local data analysts and data managers. Spatial tools that can make this process more accessible to decision makers and urban greening practitioners are needed in many cities.

Design

Our design team—Jason Kentner, partner at IMPLEMENT and associate professor of landscape architecture at Ohio State's Knowlton School, and Sean Burkholder, assistant professor of landscape and urban design at the University of Buffalo—carried out a design process to re-envision vacant lots as affordable community assets that would be sustainable in the long run. The designers worked to incorporate stormwater retention into desirable spaces for residents. Resident feedback via surveys, discussions, and community meetings shaped recreational use that was built around green stormwater infrastructure (figures 3-2 through 3-10). Each site was tailored to address the desires of the residents, within the confines of standardized components for stormwater management.

Where possible, we preserved plants, trees, and flower beds that remained from former residential use and incorporated them into the new site design. One lingering question was whether it would be possible to combine such disparate land uses in a small space without compromising either social or environmental function. (Parcels varied in size from 3,200 to 9,300 square feet.) Designers worked to minimize potential conflicts between stormwater management and recreational land uses, but this remained a central question of the Vacant to Vibrant approach.

Recreation

Through the design process, residents and community leaders were asked to think of the desired recreational function of sites along a continuum of use from passive to active. Passive spaces would provide simple places to relax or gather with neighbors and include activities such as walking, sitting, and bird-watching. Where passive spaces were desired, residents wanted peaceful, quiet spaces that would add beauty to the neighborhood. Active spaces would be used for sports and games. Where active spaces were desired, residents often spoke of the desire to have places for young children to play. In between passive and active uses were activities such as picnicking and lawn games. Recreational and environmental features were combined in the footprint of residential parcels to contain a mixture of rain gardens or bioswales and benches, picnic tables, swing sets, and, in one case, a handball court.

Because it responded to feedback from residents and stakeholders, the design approach differed among cities and from lot to lot. In Buffalo, the three properties that had been selected already had established roles and uses within the community, with one serving as a connection to an existing city park and the others occupying prominent corners where neighbors gathered. In Cleveland,

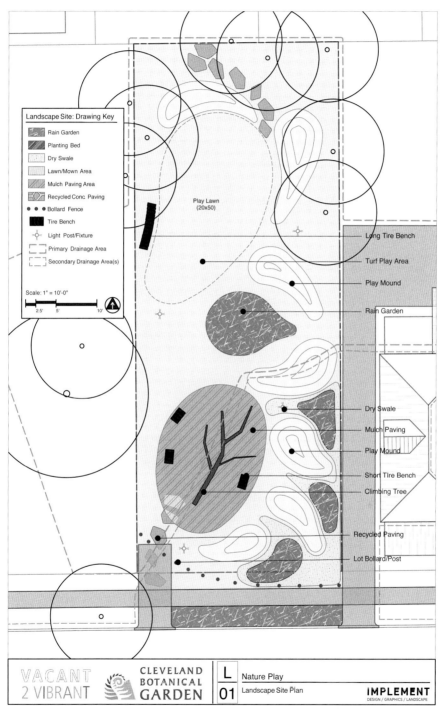

Figure 3-2. Design plan for the nature play site in Cleveland. Credit: Jason Kentner and Sean Burkholder.

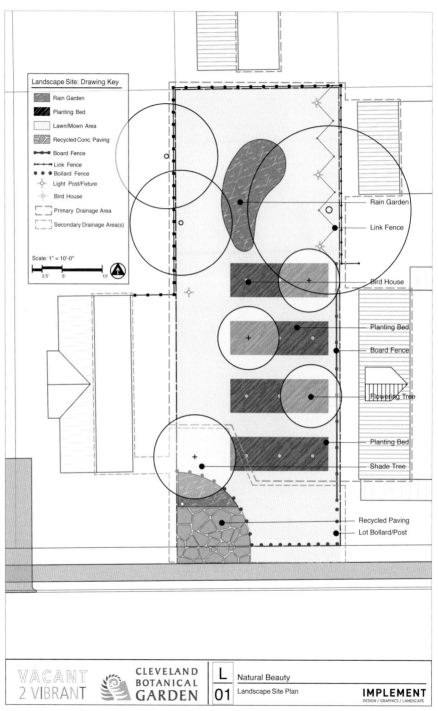

Figure 3-3. Design plan for the natural beauty site in Cleveland. Credit: Jason Kentner and Sean Burkholder.

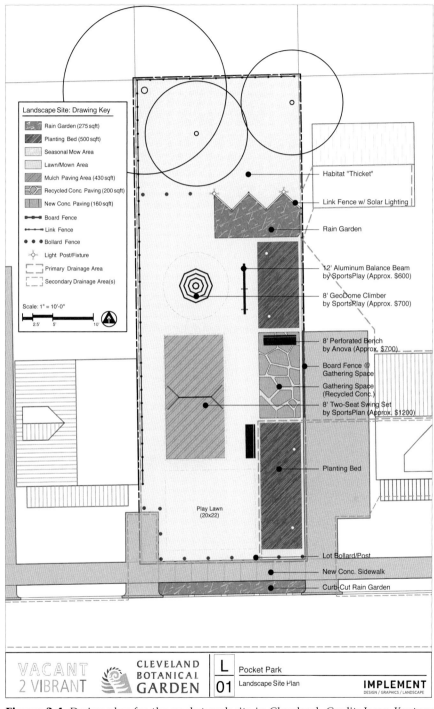

Figure 3-4. Design plan for the pocket park site in Cleveland. Credit: Jason Kentner and Sean Burkholder.

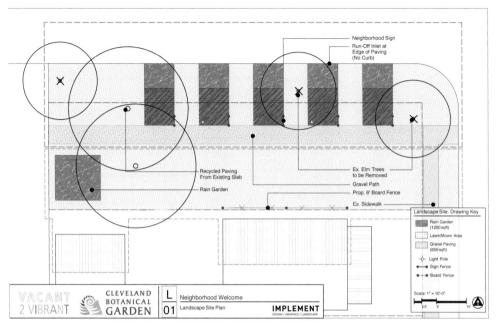

Figure 3-5. Design plan for the neighborhood welcome site in Gary. Credit: Jason Kentner and Sean Burkholder.

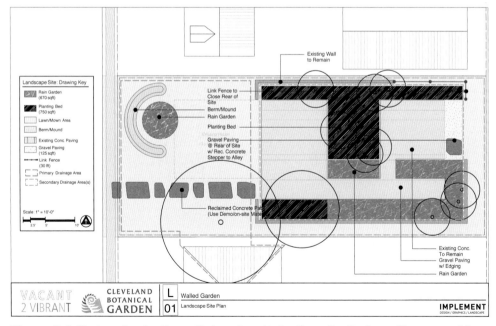

Figure 3-6. Design plan for the walled garden site in Gary. Credit: Jason Kentner and Sean Burkholder.

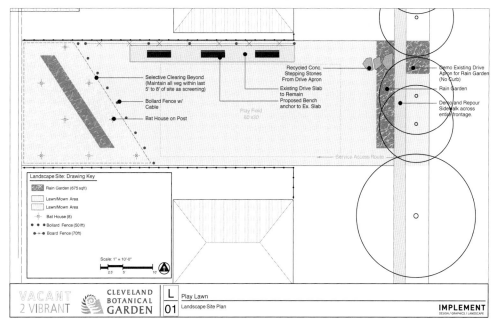

Figure 3-7. Design plan for the play lawn site in Gary. Credit: Jason Kentner and Sean Burkholder.

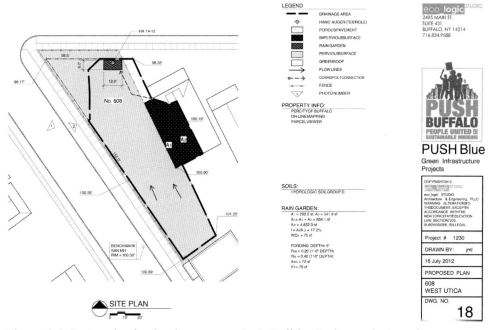

Figure 3-8. Design plan for the plant nursery site in Buffalo. Credit: eco_logic studio.

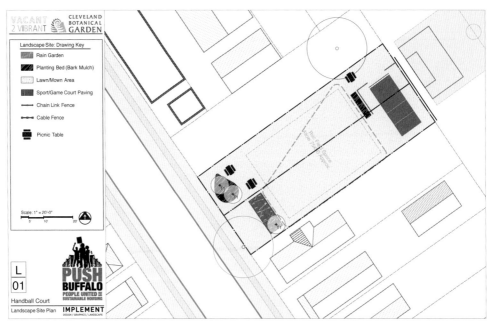

Figure 3-9. Design plan for the handball court site in Buffalo. Credit: Jason Kentner and Sean Burkholder.

we led separate planning processes with each of the three resident-led block organizations that oversaw the three streets where project sites were located. In Gary, residents wanted projects to reflect neighborhood pride but were pragmatic about the maintenance burden that sites would place on city government and residents.

Stormwater Management

Stormwater management on Vacant to Vibrant sites consisted of rain gardens planted with flowering plants, grasses, and shrubs. The number and location of the gardens varied, based on aesthetics and local conditions. At a minimum, sites were to absorb stormwater runoff that collected there so that none was contributed to combined sewer systems. In some locations where there was an opportunity for mitigation of additional stormwater runoff, designers suggested means to collect runoff from adjacent parcels or the right-of-way.

As with most stormwater best management practices, the capacity of rain gardens was assumed to be contained within the soil layer. Using stormwater management design guidelines from New York State,[3] we calculated the local drainage area based on parcel lines and adjacent impervious surfaces and estimated runoff that would be

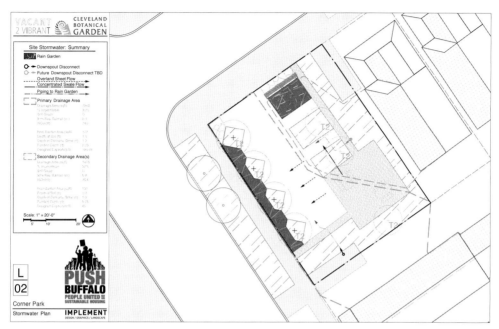

Figure 3-10. Design plan for the corner park site in Buffalo. Credit: Jason Kentner and Sean Burkholder.

generated in a one-inch stormwater event (rain or snow melt) within the area. Rain gardens were then sized to be approximately twice the size needed to contain a one-inch storm event. Even so, rain gardens did not take up a large amount of surface area, either aesthetically or in terms of interference with recreation. A more difficult challenge, however—particularly with sites that attracted more active use—was in physically separating stormwater management features within a small space, so that rain garden function would not be compromised by play. Decorative fencing and shrubs were placed to discourage active play from moving into rain gardens at sites where the two functions were near each other.

Plants

Many sites also contained plant beds for decoration that were not intended to have a significant stormwater function. For decorative beds and rain gardens, designers chose plants that would be suitable for urban environments with limited mainte-nance (table 3-5). Many of the plants chosen were natives, but we also included a small number of naturalized plants that had favorable traits. In addition to matching sun, climate, and localized soil conditions, we considered the following attributes of plants for urban vacant lots:

- *Low nutrient requirements,* so that the plants could survive in poor urban soils without fertilizer
- *Drought tolerance,* to survive hot, dry periods without supplemental water
- *Nontoxicity,* so they would not harm children or pets through contact or ingestion; particularly important when considering fruit-bearing plants
- *Herbivore tolerance,* to survive browsing from rabbits, woodchucks, and deer
- *Salt tolerance,* for areas that would be subjected to street runoff from curb cuts or road splash
- *Wildlife appeal,* to provide food or habitat for beneficial insects, birds, and wildlife
- *Noninvasiveness,* to minimize maintenance requirements, because many plants that are adapted to harsh environments can rapidly become a nuisance without adequate control
- *Visual interest* provided by flowers or foliage, to contribute to a plant "palette" that will provide visual interest throughout the year
- *Unfamiliarity,* to reduce the chance of theft, because more-recognizable plants have higher value for landscaping and may be dug up by residents or even landscapers for use at other locations
- *Moderate attractiveness,* to add beauty without becoming a target for theft, complaints, or removal

For rain gardens that received additional runoff via curb cuts or downspout disconnection, or in problematic areas of frequent standing water, we also found that *multi-stem shrubs* with open foliage soaked up additional water without obstructing sight lines through the parcel.

While it was not always possible to choose species of plants that satisfied all of these criteria, we considered location, target audience, and specific site considerations for each project to prioritize some plant characteristics over others. For example, we prioritized nontoxic plant material for pocket parks that had play equipment for small children, while herbivore tolerance and wildlife appeal were prioritized for natural areas.

Of note, plant selections for Vacant to Vibrant projects did not include many trees. At the time of project planning, trees were avoided in lieu of shrubs and shorter vegetation, in response to resident concerns about sight lines and safety, and contractor concerns about maintenance (mowing around and pruning trees). Given the current burgeoning interest in growing urban tree canopy to benefit residents and the environment, the Vacant to Vibrant project team encourages increased consideration of trees as a design element for future projects.

Table 3-5. Plants commonly used in Vacant to Vibrant projects

Type	Common name	Scientific name
Grass	Dwarf fountain grass	*Pennisetum alopecuroides* 'Hameln'
	Switchgrass	*Panicum virgatum* 'Heavy Metal'
Forb	Black-eyed Susan	*Rudbeckia fulgida*
	Daylily	*Hemerocallis* 'Stella de Oro'
	Liriope	*Liriope muscari* 'Big Blue'
	Virginia sweetspire	*Itea virginica*
	Yarrow	*Achillea millefolium*
Shrub	Sumac	*Rhus aromatica* 'Gro-Low'
	Northern bayberry	*Myrica pensylvanica*
	Inkberry holly	*Ilex glabra* 'Compacta'
	Rose of Sharon	*Hibiscus syriacus*
	Witch hazel	*Hamamelis virginiana*
	Serviceberry (multi-stem)	*Amelanchier arborea*
Tree	Pawpaw (multi-stem)	*Asimina triloba*
	Eastern redbud (multi-stem)	*Cercis canadensis*
	Red-osier dogwood	*Cornus stolonifera*
	Yellow twig dogwood	*Cornus sericea* 'Flaviramea'
	Honey locust	*Gleditsia triacanthos*
	Tulip poplar	*Liriodendron tulipifera*

Hardscape

Hardscape features included repurposed stone platforms, crushed rock pathways, benches, picnic tables, fences, birdhouses, and solar lighting. Aesthetics varied among project sites—aside from signage, there were not many common aesthetic attributes linking sites together visually. This freed us to test a variety of types and styles of materials to balance community desires, locally available materials, maintenance needs, and cost. Working with demolition contractors at one site in Gary, we were able to preserve a decorative cinder-block wall and garden patio, which easily transitioned into a community picnic spot. At another site in Gary, an intact driveway remnant was left in place to support a picnic table. In Cleveland, we were able to make use of intact fencing along perimeters of the parcels (though we removed an equal number of dilapidated fences). With future urban greening projects in these cities, it is likely that residents and project managers will establish common style elements and amenities that will then repeat across projects, but as a pilot project we enjoyed more flexibility to test a broader array of materials.

Community Engagement

Once the Vacant to Vibrant team had narrowed down potential project sites to one or two block groups of interest within a neighborhood, but before we had selected specific parcels, we began to engage community members in a planning process to develop customized designs for each site. We gathered residents' input on programming elements that would inform the use and aesthetic of each location, and the design team began to synthesize those ideas with stormwater management needs.

The focus of community engagement was providing residents with information about the purpose of the project, the construction schedule, and the need and methods for stormwater management; and to learn from them about real and potential problems in their neighborhoods that might affect project success. Dialogue with residents created new opportunities to discuss maintenance, form relationships with neighborhood leaders, and create multiple forums to discuss community issues. In Cleveland, organizing around one of our project sites further served as a catalyst for reactivating a block organization that had not met for some time prior to our project.

Community engagement was also an opportunity to recruit needed partners to the project team. We worked with local sewer authorities, community organizations, and city officials to hold public meetings, obtain permits, collaborate with local initiatives, and plan for ongoing site maintenance.

We used a variety of community engagement strategies to make decisions about site design. Although community meetings led by project leaders are a popular way of engaging residents, we frequently had poor attendance at this style of meeting, in spite of advertisements in community newsletters and door-to-door flyers. In addition, there was substantial attendance at these meetings by urban greening professionals who were staffing other community projects, which led to a low resident-to-staff ratio. (At one community meeting, we had just four residents and ten urban greening professionals in attendance.) Because of these dynamics, we did not receive as much feedback, especially candid feedback, as we did through other channels.

Collaborating with other projects increased participation in public meetings, with the downside that larger crowds were also harder to keep on topic. The most successful community meetings were organized by community leaders who had strong rapport with neighborhood residents, and were held at established community engagement outlets (such as standing monthly meetings), where we were invited guests. It was also helpful to involve community residents in planning the meeting format, choosing the speakers, and even handling details such as selecting the type of refreshments that would most appeal to residents.

Effective Personal Conversations

Community feedback was more effectively gathered through one-on-one conversations or through a liaison trusted by residents. In stoop surveys during the planning phase, we went door-to-door to houses within a five-minute walk of the site with a short questionnaire about which parks residents currently used, what types of recreational activities they would want from green space closer to home, and what feedback they had for planners of an urban greening project in their neighborhood.

Once designs were complete, we went back to residences to gather input for final tweaks to the design plans. Following advice about resident stoop surveys from Albany 2030 (an updated city plan for Albany, New York[4]), we formatted our surveys to fit on a single double-sided legal page, which we folded in half to write on. We wore casual attire and avoided the use of clipboards to reduce the chance of being mistaken for law enforcement, bill collectors, or other types of visitors that residents might want to avoid.

Other advice about successful stoop surveys that we did not implement due to staffing limitations, but that may have increased the quality of feedback, the rate of participation, or the safety of our surveyors, included sending surveyors to residences in pairs, enlisting residents to assist with surveying, and compensating residents for their time. In particular, fair compensation for residents' time is an important ethical consideration for research that involves economically disadvantaged and underrepresented groups.

If residents were unavailable to complete surveys when we knocked on their doors, we left instructions on how to access the survey online or made appointments with residents to return in person or talk by phone. Online surveys were also shared in e-newsletters, on social media, and on websites of our community partners. The response rate to online surveys was very low among our neighborhoods, which is consistent with research showing low response rates among older and low-income residents, who are less likely to have access to an internet connection at home.

Working with Community Liaisons

Another successful means of getting candid feedback was talking to residents through a trusted community liaison, whether a pastor at a local church, a community organization with an established track record in the neighborhood, or a resident in the neighborhood who could filter information back to us from neighbors. These methods worked well in combination.

For implementation teams that are not intimately knowledgeable about a neighborhood, it is necessary to get a liaison who can see the process from both perspectives. A community liaison can help reduce the time and effort needed to build and maintain a mutually trusting relationship. Building relationships takes an investment of time and energy by all sides, with redundancy needed to prepare for the likely possibility that some people will leave the project or move from the neighborhood while the project is ongoing. Additionally, this investment must be sustained over long periods of time, which requires institutional prioritization. Liaisons can help lower these barriers significantly.

A liaison was especially important to help convey negative feedback that residents were reluctant to share in direct conversation with project team members. In this way, we learned of complaints about noise, damage to neighboring properties, project appearance, and safety. We then worked with the liaison to identify a mutually satisfactory solution to each type of complaint, where possible, and to communicate timelines and progress back to the neighborhood.

Liaisons became more important when there were complications in working through a solution. In one instance, direct communication with one of our community leaders broke down, but through multiple liaisons we were able to establish additional points of contact to maintain lines of communication with residents. One downside is that negative experiences put pressure on intermediaries. At one site in Cleveland, during a prolonged period of dissatisfaction from residents about a nature play project (discussed in more detail in chapter 4), the liaison's continued involvement with us strained their relationship with residents, who were angry about the project, and eroded the residents' trust in the liaison. Such negative outcomes can reverberate to other community projects that work through the same liaison and can compromise the liaison's other work. Our experience highlights the value that should be placed on securing and preserving a liaison's trust and involvement.

Cautiously Using Word-of-Mouth

Word-of-mouth among residents was a secondary form of engagement that neighbors had with one another. This engagement between neighbors could be helpful for sharing information, with the risk that important details could be lost in a game of telephone. Neighbors who were trusted in the neighborhood were especially effective in sharing information accurately and effectively. All printed, emailed, and online materials included project team contact information to engage residents directly throughout the process; approximately 20 residents chose to contact us in this way. Sharing stacks of flyers, business cards with contact information, and other materials, as well as making repeated attempts at direct engagement, helped improve the accuracy of communication that took place directly between neighbors and encouraged direct contact between residents and project partners.

Navigating Community Politics

After our official community engagement meetings had ended in Cleveland but before the sites were constructed, the project team got wind of a community meeting that had been called on a street from which we had received little input, as it lacked a block organization. The purpose of the meeting was to discuss our upcoming projects, with the hope that residents could make changes to the location or type of project we had in the works. Most of the residents had missed our official community meetings—they had not recalled receiving a flyer at their door, or they had not been able to attend. Folks who knew about the meeting but did not attend had been skeptical in the early stages that a project would actually take place, or never cared to provide input, or had wanted to provide input but had not yet done so. Regardless, a backyard meeting in the summer at a neighbor's house on their very own street was more appealing than winter planning discussions at the local library; the meeting was very well attended.

Although the project team had not been invited, when we heard about the meeting, we asked if we could attend too, to provide information and answer questions. The informal block organization president who hosted the meeting graciously agreed. It turned out that she had planned a dinner and was delighted when we were able to reimburse costs from our meetings budget. In the end, it was a good model for us of a more effective meeting style for this particular neighborhood—working with residents directly resulted in a meeting that was better attended, with a format that was more familiar to the target audience, and with food and drink that were more suited to residents' tastes.

The meeting was a useful way to directly address false information. From the approximately 30 people present, we learned of misconceptions that had spread about our projects through rumors. We were able to give information about how designs were shaping up generally and discuss in more detail the plans for the project that would be located on their street. Of the people present, the majority opinion was that the project should feature play equipment for small children. Although we shared cautions about swing sets that we had received from other project partners, the residents felt that play equipment would be most appropriate for their street.

The meeting was also a teaching moment for the project team about neighborhood dynamics. When the meeting was over, we were afforded a glimpse into a divide in the neighborhood between homeowners and renters. A few homeowners, who tended to be older and in households without children, approached us and told us "not to worry" about the group decisions that had been made during the meeting by majority. They wanted to disregard majority opinion and see their preferences implemented—sites that were beautified but did not contain play equipment that would mainly attract children of the more transient, renting families in the neighborhood. Although we proceeded with implementation of the decisions of the majority, the meeting provided helpful context for the project team about multiple perspectives. For residents, the meeting reactivated a block organization that had fallen dormant.

Resident Concerns

As the community engagement process evolved from general information in community presentations to specific site feedback in surveys and community meetings, we moved toward agreement about recreational components that could be compatible with goals of stormwater management. Designs were adjusted to incorporate a number of resident concerns that repeated across time and across the three cities.

Safety

Early concerns from the community centered on issues of safety. Such concerns affected both overall site design and choices about individual project elements. These concerns were most pronounced in the Gary and Cleveland neighborhoods, where residents had little prior experience with reuse of vacant parcels and were concerned that the sites would attract unwanted visitors from within and outside the neighborhoods. Residents were specifically interested in reducing the attractiveness of the sites to teens and young adults for the purposes of gambling, drinking and drug use, loitering, and violence.

Every element of each site design was evaluated through a lens of safety: Would vegetation harbor criminals, rodents, or pests? Would there be standing water in the rain garden for mosquitoes? Could children get hurt? Would there be adequate lighting after dark? Would there be fencing along the perimeters of the parcel so that people engaged in unwanted activity could not easily run through the site?

Smooth, hard surfaces had to be broken up to discourage gambling. To preserve sight lines across project sites, we kept plant cover sparse above three-foot heights in all locations. In Cleveland, residents requested that we remove a bench that had been included in design plans for one of the sites, lest it encourage loitering. Every design element of the projects was evaluated first with an eye toward how it would influence actual or perceived safety within the neighborhood.

Vandalism

Resident concerns about vandalism included fears that people would dismantle, destroy, or deface equipment on the site, as well as that people would use materials on the site to damage neighboring properties. Residents and community partners in all three cities requested that equipment be made vandalism-proof by bolting it down, adding a paint-resistant coating, or using durable materials that would have no resale value and that could not be easily broken. In Buffalo, design elements that included rocks of a size that could be easily thrown were rejected by our community partner, due to past negative experiences. (As discussed later, we made one exception to this rule in Cleveland.)

Scrapping and salvaging metal, wood, plants, and other materials with resale value is common in many urban communities. To the extent possible, we used materials that would not be likely to be removed for these purposes. Copper components on our monitoring equipment were buried in concrete, and exposed parts were spray-painted green. For fencing, light posts, benches, and other metal components, we used steel in lieu of aluminum, due to its lower value for scrap. We considered the theft value of trees and plants too, and opted for plants that were not as recognizable to the general public, excluding popular species such as azalea, rhododendron, rose, and flowering trees in favor of decorative grasses and less commonly recognized plants. (Low theft appeal is one seldom-touted advantage of native plants in urban areas.)

Crime

Residents preferred park equipment that was very juvenile in appearance, to discourage older youth from wanting to use it. Hours of restricted use were to be posted on signage to provide residents and law enforcement with a reason to clear the sites after dark.

As we received this extensive feedback about safety, we had to weigh lessons that had been well established in other cities against residents' long-standing experience in their own neighborhoods. In Gary and Cleveland, we shared with residents findings from other cities showing that improvements to vacant lots tended to reduce—not increase—the incidence of crime. For example, in Philadelphia, researchers studying the LandCare program of the Pennsylvania Horticultural Society observed a decrease in violent crime on vacant lots.[5] The researchers hypothesized that this decrease was due to several factors, including a greater perception of care, a more beneficial use of the sites that discourages people from illegal activities, and the higher visibility of parcels and clearer sight lines across them, as well as the possibility of reductions in stress among neighborhood residents. The researchers did notice an increase in petty crime charges (such as public intoxication), however, due to greater use of the sites and higher rates of reporting crime, which was concerning for residents in Gary and Cleveland.

In general, residents in Gary and Cleveland neighborhoods that had little experience with urban greening practices were reluctant to accept findings from other cities. Given the lack of formal research about the effects of vacant lot improvement projects, it remains unknown whether Gary and Cleveland neighborhoods differ significantly from areas where the effects of urban greening have been investigated. Comparisons between these cities and Buffalo suggest that community improvements may be perceptible to residents only after a number of vacant land projects have taken place. Findings from Buffalo also show the value of having knowledgeable community partners, who can head off resident concerns by intervening early around known sensitive topics. Concerns about crime, whether real or perceived, heavily influenced resident engagement for urban greening projects at Vacant to Vibrant project sites.

Connectivity

Although connectivity is often cited by city planners as a design feature that strengthens projects and neighborhoods, residents voiced fears that connecting the sides and back of projects to adjacent vacant lots or yards would create points of entry and exit that could be used for crime. In Cleveland, residents shared stories about youth running through yards with guns as part of gang-related activities. In Gary, residents feared that connecting one project to an abutting parcel along a main thoroughfare would aid burglaries and other property crime. We addressed these concerns by preserving fences along the sides and backs of parcels where possible, and by adding more fences, particularly in the back of lots, at select sites in Cleveland and Gary.

Appearance and Intended Audience

As the design process progressed, feedback moved to issues of appearance and intended audience of the parks. Residents favored more commonly known plants over native plants for their appearance, but native plants won out with the project team for their lower maintenance and lower aesthetic appeal for theft. Feedback from PUSH Buffalo suggested that reducing the number of plant species to about four per project area, and grouping individual species into rows or clusters, improved residents' opinion of their appearance, with the added benefit for many contractors of making plants easier to distinguish from weeds in the spring. To increase biodiversity over the entire project area, assemblages of species could then be varied across neighboring beds or project sites.

Nature play and recycled elements—used successfully at Holden Forests & Gardens' Hershey Children's Garden and other public gardens to inspire creative play—were less desirable to residents than traditional park equipment. The project team was interested in using natural elements such as play logs, hills, and repurposed objects to encourage connections with nature and convey project themes of sustainability. During the design phase, some residents expressed doubts that children growing up in a very urbanized environment would intuitively understand how to interact with a nature play park theme, though the design was eventually approved by the majority. As explained in the next chapter, these concerns of the minority foreshadowed pain and resentment that would lead to dramatic design modifications of the nature play lot after installation.

When it came to recreational use of the sites and the intended beneficiaries of parks, most residents favored equipment that could be used by young children and elderly residents. Equipment for adults, such as gym equipment and walking paths, was less popular. The least popular among residents was any feature that was considered to be attractive to older youth, due to concerns about drug activity, loitering, and undesirable activity.

Maintenance Capacity

An additional concern among residents in Gary and Cleveland was about maintenance capacity—whether adequate capacity existed to maintain urban greening projects, and whether that maintenance would be stable in the long term (discussed in greater detail in chapter 5). These fears were directly linked to examples of municipal parks in Gary and vacant land use projects in Cleveland that had fallen into disrepair over time due to lack of funding or changes in responsibility or liability. In general, residents were cautious about adding anything that had obvious maintenance requirements, such as sport courts.

Neighborhood-Specific Community Engagement Lessons

While there was significant overlap among the three Vacant to Vibrant cities in concerns and needs for urban greening, there were some points of divergence in lessons from each neighborhood. We customized community engagement methods and schedules to fit the needs and circumstances of each of the three neighborhoods.

Aetna, Gary

Beautification and revitalization were popular design themes among Aetna residents. This part of the Aetna neighborhood, west of Aetna Street, is home to mostly older residents and is a quiet area—and the desire to keep it so was pervasive. During stoop surveys, the majority of residents voiced a desire to design projects for passive use, opting against specific programming like sports or active play. A community meeting reiterated much the same sentiment and helped to solidify consensus on designs. The sites' lighting, natural areas, walking paths, and trails were all aimed at increasing safety and beauty. Community picnic tables were planned for two sites but would be available only with advance coordination with city government (free of charge). In the final round of design, personal mailers were sent to residents within 150 feet of each project site, leading to a half-dozen follow-up phone calls. Final phone discussions about the Aetna sites were positive, requiring no significant design changes.

Woodland Hills, Cleveland

In Cleveland, resident interests in recreation ranged more widely. An introductory community engagement meeting took place jointly with the Northeast Ohio Regional Sewer District and the Trust for Public Land, giving the project team an opportunity to introduce the Vacant to Vibrant project and its relationship to other green infrastructure projects. Though the meeting was only lightly attended by residents, key neighborhood leaders came to learn about the project and other green infrastructure projects nearby and conveyed this information to their neighbors. The first round of stoop surveys during the summer also revealed a wide variety of desires among residents, from active uses such as sport courts and natural play areas, to passive uses such as sitting areas and reflective spaces.

A well-attended community design input meeting in the middle of the planning process allowed residents to focus on specific sites and to narrow the range of proposed site design themes. Residents near two of the sites preferred active use, while the third group strongly emphasized more passive use. A community design feedback meeting a month later gave residents a chance to review plan updates that incorporated previous discussions and surveys. Because some residents near the project sites were not in attendance, a final follow-up survey of all residents within 150 feet helped solidify design input. Response to the design for the passive site was not as high as for the two active sites, for which the details of the design (such as connection to rear parcels and safety via lighting) were of greater concern to neighbors.

Concerns about the active play site sparked a block organization meeting to address specific design features. Much of the concern centered on the image of a basketball hoop that was used as a placeholder to symbolize an as-yet-undecided active recreational use in an early artistic rendering of design plans. We had already been warned against amenities that would attract older youth, due to concerns about drugs and violence, so we had no plans for a basketball court at this site. We had not realized the loaded symbolism of the basketball hoop, however, and the image in the early renderings had to be changed before we could proceed with meaningful conversation about any active use of the site.

These worries were reignited later by the suggestion of a young children's ball funnel, which residents felt would be too tempting to use in a way that resembled basketball (figure 3-11). Picnic tables in the artistic rendering also drew criticism over their perceived attractiveness to older youth, though most residents remained open to encouraging some degree of activity and congregation on the parcel.

In general, community engagement in Cleveland taught the design team that residents may look at artistic renderings as being literal representations of what is to be constructed on the site, even if the renderings were not created to relay literal intent. In retrospect, structuring engagement around design plans, which did reflect literal intent, would have yielded more productive conversation among residents about

Figure 3-11. Artistic rendering of the design plan for the pocket park site in Cleveland. The portrayal of the children's ball game, meant as a conversation starter for community engagement about active play, replaced an earlier rendering that showed a basketball hoop. It still caused concern among residents, however, who worried about attracting older youth. Credit: Jason Kentner and Sean Burkholder.

specific project elements, possibly avoiding the disappointment that occurred later with the nature play site. A drawback to relying on design plans alone is the educational barrier to their interpretation—since they are abstract, they require adequate time for detailed explanation.

Key design elements that emerged for all the sites in Cleveland included safety concerns, options for children, maintenance, restricting hours of use, and mitigating illegal activity. The need to create a net benefit for the community, balancing neighborhood assets and liabilities, was a consistent theme in Cleveland's resident feedback.

West Side, Buffalo

Because of PUSH's long-standing community involvement, community engagement for the Vacant to Vibrant project on Buffalo's West Side was structured differently than in Cleveland and Gary. Unlike partners in the other cities, PUSH had already identified specific project sites at the time of the first community engagement meeting, allowing meetings to address specific design considerations from the outset. Door-to-door canvassing, monthly community development committee meetings, an annual planning congress, and virtual conversations through social media were already a part of PUSH's activities, so the concept and pitch of Vacant to Vibrant was incorporated into their established operations.

At two of the three project sites, ongoing conversations and outreach led to an early consensus on having an active space adjacent to a park and another place to congregate. Canvassing and development meetings over the summer helped confirm specific elements of each site by polling nearby residents and providing an open door for input about programming.

Community Engagement's Role in Shaping Resident Expectations

As project implementation progressed in each of the three cities, the project team observed how resident expectations might have scaled with the level of community engagement. While the project team used best practices for community engagement, in hopes of including as many residents as possible, we also observed that increased engagement inadvertently suggested to residents that project scopes were bigger than they actually were, or that residents would have more control over the projects than they actually would. This led us to question whether it was possible to "overengage" residents.

In Cleveland, we shared early community meetings with the regional sewer authority, which was constructing a $5 million green infrastructure project to mitigate 17 million gallons of stormwater per year in the neighborhood. Although we were transparent about the modest costs of our project relative to others', the Vacant to Vibrant team was involved in the community at a level that appeared to be disproportionate with project costs, based on norms that had been established by larger projects in the neighborhood. For some residents, freedom to shape recreational use set up unrealistic expectations about their level of control over other aspects of the project. Other residents voiced disappointment that the projects were more modest than they had expected. Some residents involved in planning the nature play project in Cleveland petitioned to remove stormwater management from the project to free up more of the project's budget for recreation. These problems were not as pronounced in Gary, where we had fewer meetings, or in Buffalo, where discussions about Vacant to Vibrant were grouped with other neighborhood initiatives.[6]

Vacant to Vibrant engaged residents with the hope that feedback could be incorporated into a number of future community greening projects. Future projects might consider curbing disappointment by more narrowly focusing discussions. Approaching residents with a more limited menu of vetted design options, drawing on lessons about projects that work well (and those that do not), and coordinating with other initiatives that are similar in scope may avoid inflating resident expectations beyond what the project can deliver. At the same time, as this type of community investment becomes more common, residents will benefit from more familiarity with urban greening projects, reducing chances for confusion.

Lessons Learned

Planning to convert vacant residential parcels to stormwater parks consisted of iterative processes for choosing sites, drafting site plans that married recreation and stormwater management, and collecting resident feedback. A top-down process for site selection, beginning with all available parcels and narrowing them down to project sites using sets of suitability criteria, is technically challenging but allows urban greening practitioners to efficiently choose sites that fit project objectives. Widespread adoption of top-down site selection processes will be needed to achieve cost-effective stormwater management at larger scales. When urban greening practitioners have flexibility in choosing project sites, it is helpful to partner with data analysts in the absence of accessible spatial tools. As spatial analysis becomes more commonly taught at the undergraduate college level, this expertise is becoming more widely available.

Designing urban greening projects that prioritize social and environmental benefits requires deft balancing of competing needs, with the potential payoff that multi-benefit projects can be an efficient use of space and funding for neighborhood stabilization.

Without established best practices for projects like Vacant to Vibrant, flexibility, creativity, and experimentation are key. The project team placed special emphasis on keeping projects' maintenance requirements low, in accordance with the lower maintenance capacity typical of neighborhoods with abundant vacant land.

Community engagement throughout the design process that provided multiple means and methods of communication yielded valuable resident feedback that, in turn, shaped project design. Meeting residents where they live—whether at established meetings or on their front porches—was the most successful means of engagement in terms of number and diversity of residents reached. Where project teams are not closely associated with the community, having trusted community members or organizations as liaisons is critical for bridging gaps between project team members and residents within a typically short project timeline. A future consideration for community engagement is making more efficient use of residents' time by offering them choices from among a more limited menu of options that have been vetted for suitability for an urban greening project and that otherwise meet project objectives and budget.

4

Vacant to Vibrant Implementation

Preparation for installing the Vacant to Vibrant projects began in the later stages of the design process, after the sites were finalized. There were permits to obtain, timelines to coordinate, and agreements to draft to formalize leases, contractors, and community partners. Construction began in fall 2014, in the third year of the project, and extended through spring 2015 (see appendix). The extensive preparatory work of selecting sites and creating detailed agreements paid off in this next phase of the project—once ground was broken, installation proceeded relatively smoothly. No costly surprises were hidden under the soil surface of parcels, and no major incidents disrupted work. This translated to projects that were built to specification, within the expected time frame, close to original budgeted costs (table 4-1).

The ease of installation belied the difficulties that would arise afterward, particularly in Cleveland with the two active play projects. Looking back, hiccups that had taken place during planning, particularly around design elements that had sparked resident disagreement, foreshadowed the difficulty that followed after projects were completed. Given the experimental nature of the project, we were fortunate to have been able to allocate additional resources to modify project sites to address problem areas; this is not usually possible. Modifications to the two projects to address resident feedback and issues such as vandalism proceeded over the next two years. With the benefit of hindsight, these experiences emphasized the need to plan for both contingency funding and an iterative construction process for experimental urban projects such as Vacant to Vibrant.

Table 4-1. Vacant to Vibrant project summaries

Project		Size (sq ft)	Recreational Use		Cost[a]	Cost/gallon[b]	
						Storm-water	CSO
	Nature play	6,292	Active	Swing, bench	$13,531	$0.09	$0.88
Cleveland	Natural beauty	4,346	Passive	Birdhouses	17,653	0.17	1.66
	Pocket park	4,590	Active	Bench, swing, balance beam	19,004	0.17	1.70
	Neighbor-hood welcome	4,368	Passive	Path, neighbor-hood sign	20,777	0.19	1.95
Gary	Walled garden	6,575	Light active	Picnic table	16,819	0.10	1.05
	Play lawn	5,148	Active	Picnic table, play lawn, bat houses	14,007	0.11	1.12
	Plant nursery	5,168	Passive	Path, plant nursery	8,827	0.06	0.58
Buffalo	Handball court	9,271	Active	Picnic tables, handball court	35,305	0.15	1.51
	Corner park	3,203	Light active	Bench, pervious parking, path	8,827	0.08	0.80

[a] Installation costs. Costs for two Buffalo projects were averaged after they were billed jointly.

[b] Cost per gallon of stormwater capture based on precipitation in a typical year (NOAA, 1981–2010) and assumed 10 gallons of stormwater capture to mitigate 1 gallon of Combined Sewer Overflow (CSO) (average from NEORSD, 2012).

This chapter will examine the implementation process and the resultant nine Vacant to Vibrant projects in detail, offering guidance about how to approach similar projects in any neighborhood. Modifications to original designs took place for a variety of reasons, some of which can be instructive for urban greening projects that are intended for neighborhood stabilization. Because native plant material makes up a large portion of the project budget for these and other urban greening projects, the project team constructed plant nurseries in Gary and Buffalo to provide a local, affordable source for plant material in the future; the format and partners for these nurseries can serve as models in cities where there is a need and capacity to grow plants for urban greening projects.

Project Installation

Once parcels were chosen for the project sites, we established written agreements with project partners, engaged contractors, and assessed installation requirements for each site in preparation for breaking ground.

Written Agreements

After vacant parcels were selected for project sites, we began the process of drafting agreements that outlined their intended use and sought permission to access them for the purposes of project installation and maintenance. In Cleveland, where vacant parcels were owned by the city land bank, city government had a predefined lease process for site access covering five-year increments. Applications to lease parcels in Cleveland included a review of site plans, a maintenance plan, and a $1-per-parcel application fee.

In Gary and Buffalo, where parcel owners were members of the project team (city government and the community organization People United for Sustainable Housing [PUSH], respectively) and would assume maintenance of projects after installation, a memorandum of understanding replaced a formal lease agreement. In each agreement, the Cleveland Botanical Garden was named as one party (as project team leader), and the landowner was named as the second party. Each agreement followed the same format: It first outlined the purpose of Vacant to Vibrant and the nature of the relationship between the two parties as collaborators. Then it separately outlined the responsibilities of each party, including access to specific parcels, project tasks, any exchange of compensation for time or expenses, and a general timeline for completion. At the conclusion of the agreement were details about liability, expectations for communication, an outline of how elements in the document could be modified as needed, and other responsibilities shared by both parties.

Although the process of drafting a custom agreement between parties was somewhat time consuming and required the added expense of legal oversight, the agreements helped ensure clarity and fairness to both parties and clearly spelled out the
nature of their collaboration. If a project team member had needed to leave the project, for instance, the written agreement would have helped ensure continuity within
the project team. The project team benefited from donated time from a volunteer
with nonprofit legal expertise, who was able to guide us in drafting the agreements
for approval by legal counsel.

Contractor Engagement

In each city, we selected landscaping crews that had extensive experience with installation and maintenance of sustainable land use practices such as rain gardens, bioswales, downspout disconnections, and native plants. When we solicited proposals
for contractors, we asked for ability and experience in both landscape and general
contracting (or the ability to subcontract within budget requirements) to handle
installation of plantings and hardscape, as well as a locally sourced workforce and
direct experience with stormwater management techniques. In Gary, our request
included an additional provision to work with the city's newly formed Urban Conservation Team, who would assume maintenance of Vacant to Vibrant sites and other
city parks, to perform unskilled tasks and to allow them to observe technical aspects
of project installation.

Due to the specificity of our requests and a modest project budget (installation
contracts averaged $54,000 per city), it was a challenge to receive a sufficient number
of qualified bids. In Cleveland, we received one qualified quote that fell within our
specifications, from a small landscape contractor, based in the neighborhood, who
had worked on diverse landscaping projects throughout the city and region. In Gary,
we issued two rounds of requests for quotes before receiving a satisfactory quote from
a small landscape contractor from a neighboring city. PUSH employed its own team
of trained landscape contractors with such experience, so their team installed the
projects in Buffalo.

In the end, the competitive bids came from small, local contracting companies who saw potential in advancing their skills in stormwater best management
practices. With the exception of the handball court in Buffalo and tree removal
in Gary, which were subcontracted, and signage in Buffalo and Gary, which was
installed by the companies that fabricated the signs, these small landscaping
firms handled all aspects of project installation. Although it took effort to find
contractors who could meet a long list of requirements, the result was three

companies that were invested in project outcomes and that were enjoyable to work with.

The overlap between installation and maintenance personnel in Buffalo and Gary would impact the quality of maintenance in the following three years. With PUSH being involved in early stages of project planning, they were able to work directly with the design team to ensure that site designs would include plants and materials that PUSH could grow or source locally, to make sure that finished projects would fit with the maintenance capacity of their team, and to head off any potential problem areas with residents. In Gary, the city's Urban Conservation Team worked directly with the contractor during installation to understand the construction and maintenance requirements of rain gardens, which prepared them for eventual maintenance of the area's Vacant to Vibrant projects.

The benefits of continuity in working relationships through installation and maintenance were underlined in Cleveland, where the installation contractor turned over maintenance to another neighborhood-based landscape contractor after the project build. Having not had the opportunity to learn about project goals and help shape the design, the new maintenance contractor struggled to understand the dual goals—stormwater management and recreation—of the project; additionally, he was unsure how to thin the beds of native plants that had matured and shifted in species composition after installation. As a result, the sites looked increasingly different from the original designs over time. This contractor had a better sense of the types of plants that neighbors would enjoy, however; the project would have benefited from his earlier input and involvement.

Installation Overview

All nine parcels had been demolished and graded to become relatively flat vacant lots at the time of installation. Two parcels in Gary had vacant homes on them at the time of installation. The City of Gary demolished these homes using federal Hardest Hit funding and left them as graded vacant parcels, minus the addition of grass seed, which would normally be included in a post-demolition site finish.

In the footprint of each rain garden, soil was excavated to a two-foot depth. Holes were first backfilled with one foot of coarse rock, which contains ample pore space to store runoff below the soil surface. On top of the rock, we placed one foot of an engineered bioinfiltration soil mix composed of nearly half sand and little clay, to quickly infiltrate water from the surface, and 20 to 30 percent leaf compost to support plant establishment. These subsurface layers of a rain garden infiltrate runoff from the surface within 24 hours of a one-inch rainfall or snowmelt to reduce the risk of standing water on the parcel.

Drains were incorporated into design plans, but they were not installed. By the time design plans had been approved, city engineers in Buffalo (where drains had been more of a concern than in the other two cities) had gained enough experience with green stormwater infrastructure that their opinions about required overflow capacity had changed. The project team determined that the rain gardens were sized generously enough that the sites would rarely have enough standing water at such depths to require drains, and city engineers agreed.

Once the rain gardens were backfilled to match the surface grade of each parcel, they were capped with hardwood bark mulch and then planted. Because not much scientific information exists about the role that evaporation and transpiration from plants play in stormwater management, the plants were assumed to have a decorative role only. This assumption provided latitude in the types of plants that could be used in the design of stormwater parks. As described in chapter 3, we chose plants that had low maintenance requirements, that fit with plans for recreational use, and that were otherwise suited to urban vacant lots.

Lawn portions of each lot were planted in a full-sun lawn mix in Gary and Buffalo and, in Cleveland, in a low-maintenance lawn mix. Lawn was slow to establish when direct-sown into vacant lot soil without soil amendments. Having learned from the experience of other vacant land use projects conducted by Holden Forests & Gardens, we have had better success with lawn cover, including lower weed content, when sowing lawn seed into a layer of one to two inches of leaf humus, which adds nutrients and water-holding capacity to nurture young grass seedlings. Of note, lawn mixes that are branded as "low-maintenance" or "low-mow" have specific requirements for sowing that must be strictly followed for good results. If the instructions of such mixes cannot be followed to the letter, including planting in the fall (or in the very early spring if using other weed control measures), then we recommend using a traditional lawn mix in place of low-mow mixes to achieve adequate lawn cover with low urban weed composition.

⊛ ⊛ ⊛ ⊛ ⊛ ⊛ ⊛ ⊛ ⊛ ⊛ ⊛

Vacant to Vibrant Project Descriptions

Cleveland Project Descriptions

On three quiet, parallel residential streets in the Woodland Hills neighborhood, residents wanted urban green spaces that beautified the neighborhood and provided play opportunities for young children.

Site 1: Nature Play

On this quiet residential street, residents and block organization leaders homed in on an active play concept that would appeal to young children. A few parcels down, children had tied a used tire onto a small tree with rope, building for themselves the only swing set on the block.

The final design was a nature play area, conceived as a whimsical and environmentally sustainable alternative to traditional park equipment (figure 4-1). A series of grassy play mounds framed one side of the parcel. In the front, a swale consisting of rain gardens and round, river-washed gravel flowed around the play mounds like a dry creek bed. Two additional rain gardens, one in the rear of the parcel and one in the grassy strip by the street, collected additional runoff. One of the main features of the nature play site was a play log. By coincidence, a tree 18 inches in diameter, which met design specifications, had fallen onto the parcel in a storm that took place during the construction period. Given that it was freshly fallen, sound, and had a history with the parcel, this seemed to be the perfect play log. Its branches were cut back to a two-inch diameter, and the log was anchored by rebar into a bed of soft mulch. Benches, formed from rows of repurposed tires that were sunken into the ground, surrounded the play log and doubled as bouncing and climbing structures.

To our disappointment, when construction was completed there was an outcry about the nature play concept from residents and the block organization leader. This was surprising, because stoop surveys and community meetings about the design had not previously captured such negative feedback about the site plans; it appeared to go beyond normal disagreement. Of course we were shocked by the overwhelmingly negative feedback, and at first did not understand why it was so severe.

Upon visiting the site after the final components—the play log and tire benches—had been put into place, however, it was obvious that the neighborhood context completely altered how the design translated into reality, in ways the project team had failed to anticipate. In the context of a declining neighborhood at 60 percent occupancy, with many vacant lots and poorly kept houses, the play log and tire benches too closely resembled

Figure 4-1a. (left) The residential vacant lot that would become the nature play site in Cleveland.

Figure 4-1b. (below) The finished nature play site featured lawn mounds, a play log, and repurposed tires as benches/play structures.

common eyesores in the neighborhood. The play log looked like numerous fallen logs that could be found on vacant lots in the neighborhood. Due to financial constraints that create a slow response rate for removal, fallen trees can remain on vacant lots for months or years in Cleveland. The tires that had been repurposed as benches and bouncing structures too closely resembled dumped tires that are also common to vacant lots, where dumping allows people to escape disposal fees. In other feedback that had not surfaced during planning, residents strongly associated tires with standing water and mosquitoes, in spite of measures taken to prevent standing water from collecting in the tires by sinking the bottom halves below ground.

Problems that were obvious in person had been missed during a lengthy design phase. The intent of the recycled features was to be sustainable, inspire creative play, and connect kids with nature. Although repurposed materials have been used successfully in several public children's gardens, residents in this Cleveland neighborhood felt hurt that their project had been built using reclaimed materials, which they felt were of lower value than new park equipment. Feedback we received on the finished nature play design included "It is made from trash" and "Our children are from the city; they have no idea how to use this!"

An additional contributing factor was that, in our community engagement process, we did not engage residents from one street in discussion about projects that were to be built on other streets. Within this small neighborhood, however, it did not take long for residents to notice that traditional park equipment had been freshly installed as part of the Vacant to Vibrant pocket park installation three streets away. This contrast added to negative feelings about the nature play park. The block organization leader felt so hurt and betrayed that she refused to talk with us directly, telling us instead to speak to her through community liaisons. In turn, liaisons felt pressure from residents, which lowered the currency of trust that they had carefully cultivated. Almost immediately after construction was finished, we began another round of community engagement to plan for site modifications.

Site 2: Natural Beauty

This vacant residential parcel stood among homes of mostly senior residents who were interested in adding value to their street but wanted to maintain a quiet atmosphere. Prior to the installation, the parcel was a simple, grassy vacant lot. The concept for this installation was a passive natural area, to both appeal to older homeowners and beautify the neighborhood (figure 4-2). At the front of the parcel, a decorative hard surface was built using recycled paving stones. An adjacent rain garden collected runoff from the surface and the front of the parcel. Earlier plans to include a bench at the front of the parcel were scrapped due to resident concerns about loitering. On the body of the parcel, four parallel planting beds were filled with a variety of tall flowering forbs, decorative grasses, shrubs, and birdhouses. A bollard fence in front of the parcel provided a decorative border that doubled as a deterrent to parking and dumping.

Three years after installation, the site has remained similar to its original design. Over time, the composition of native plants in the parallel planting beds has shifted; plants have filled in, and some decorative flowering plants have been gradually edged out by other vegetation. These are common and anticipated changes that take place with native plantings, which require cultivation to maintain a tidy, bunched appearance that is more acceptable to residents. In addition, over the three-year period, most of the birdhouses have remained unoccupied, and on two occasions several have been knocked off their posts by vandals. For these reasons, future modifications may include removal of the birdhouses from the installation.

Figure 4-2a. (left) The Cleveland natural beauty site before construction.

Figure 4-2b. (below) The natural beauty site, with birdhouses in beds of native flowers, was designed to beautify the neighborhood and provide a space for quiet reflection.

Site 3: Pocket Park

There was a dearth of play equipment for young children in this neighborhood. There was no park within walking distance, and most of the homes were owned by seniors or landlords. The neighbors reported gang-related activity from a housing development just to the north, an area separated from this quiet residential street by fencing with no cross streets, so they wanted a design that would look too juvenile to attract older youth. The existing vacant lot was simple: a patch of land overgrown with grass, next to houses owned by senior residents, who were interested in outdoor play opportunities for their grandchildren, and houses rented by younger families with children.

The final design for this play site contained a swing set sized for young children and a simple metal balance beam (figure 4-3). A hard surface composed of reused stone paving invited children to gather, perform, or play; made of broken pavers and spaced with fine gravel, the surface was also designed to discourage use of dice for gambling by older youth. Two benches provided a spot for parents, grandparents, and older residents to sit and watch children. Toward the back of the parcel, a rain garden was bordered by a short, decorative chain link fence with solar lighting. A rain garden in the city-owned lawn strip between sidewalk and street collected street runoff.

Modifications to this parcel over time included mowing a naturalized low-mow area at the rear of the lot, due to concerns about safety and aesthetics from residents. Early plans for a ball-tossing game, where balls could be thrown into a large bin and emerge randomly from one of four holes at the bottom, were rejected by residents out of fear that the game would be used like a basketball hoop by older youth. Similarly, a geodome climber included in the original design was not installed because of safety concerns about children climbing and older youth congregating.

Figure 4-3a. (left) The Cleveland pocket park site before construction.

Figure 4-3b. (below) The pocket park, with a swing set, a balance beam, and a paved pad that could serve as a stage, filled a void in this neighborhood, which was located outside walking distance to a park.

The site was overwhelmingly successful in attracting young children for play while not attracting older youth. Destructive play was also common, however, and was the major reason for site modifications, resulting in eventual removal of broken solar lighting and interpretive signage. Swing set chains were replaced multiple times due to breakage and possibly intentional cutting. To withstand heavy foot traffic, plants were replaced with decorative sumac in the rear rain garden and turf grass in the right-of-way.

Gary Project Descriptions

In the Aetna neighborhood of Gary, residents were interested in adding beautification and low-key leisure space to their quiet residential community.

Site 1: Neighborhood Welcome

In Gary, one turn off the main artery into the Aetna neighborhood—aptly named Aetna Street—sat a windowless, red-with-white-trim bungalow at the corner of East 12th Avenue and Oklahoma Street, obscured by heavy foliage. It had been vacant for longer than most residents of the neighborhood could remember—15 to 20 years, at least. None of the current residents could remember who had last lived there. This house was first on a long list of demolitions planned for Aetna by the City of Gary using Hardest Hit funds. The vacant house was overgrown with tall weeds and woody plants. Along the sidewalk flanking the house on two sides were a number of tall ash trees showing signs of emerald ash borer infestation.

Although the community of Aetna predated Gary, there was no marker at its borders telling visitors they had crossed into a historic neighborhood. The design plan naturally gravitated toward signage that announced the neighborhood name with pride (figure 4-4). Cars approaching the parcel from the east would see five signs, one in each of five rain gardens, spelling out A-E-T-N-A in a series of attractive signs made of perforated metal in wooden frames. A path of fine gravel led off the sidewalk along the side of each of the signs. A slight hill ran down the length of the parcel, subtly dividing it into two small drainage areas that each led to separate rain gardens. Three years post-installation, the site remains close to the original design plans.

Site 2: Walled Garden

This site was one of two parcels that contained vacant houses at the start of the project. The houses were demolished in collaboration with the City of Gary using Hardest Hit funds. One advantage of working with demolition contractors was the ability to preserve features of the old property that could be repurposed for community benefit, and this site

Figure 4-4a. (left) This house in Gary had stood vacant for 15 to 20 years prior to Vacant to Vibrant.

Figure 4-4b. (below) On this prominent corner at an entry point into the neighborhood, visitors are welcomed to Aetna. Each letter sign sits within a small rain garden. Credit: Cooley's Video

was a great example. Behind the house was an expansive patio garden containing trees, beds, and a decorative cinder-block wall. These features were preserved in the final project design of a quiet public garden and picnicking spot (figure 4-5). Approximately half of the plant beds were converted to rain gardens to provide more belowground storage volume for stormwater runoff from the concrete patio. A path was added to connect the sidewalk to the patio, and a rain garden in the front of the parcel captured additional runoff from the patio and the gently sloping lawn. A berm in front of the rain garden interrupted runoff flow, capturing stormwater.

The rear of the parcel had a break in the cinder-block wall for access to the old garage. The garage structure was demolished with the house, but the break in the wall remained and became a point of contention for the neighbor across the street who, after the demolition of the house, was troubled by the clear sight line to the street beyond. He feared that the break in the wall would open up the street to foot traffic from the main thoroughfare. We

Figure 4-5a. (left) Behind this vacant house in Gary, a garden patio with a decorative cinder-block wall in the backyard was still in good shape.

Figure 4-5b. (below) The finished walled garden site provides a picnicking and gathering spot for residents, with a rain garden in the footprint of the demolished house. (Picnic table delivered by the City of Gary on request.) Credit: Cooley's Video

discussed different possible compromises to keep the connection between streets open while restricting sight lines. At first, the City of Gary agreed to place a gate across the wall opening, with a lock that they would retain the right to open at a later date. Later they realized that constructing a wall would set an unrealistic precedent for future neighborhood demolitions, most of which would not come with funding to construct rear fences or walls in the back of parcels. After reviewing adjacent parcels that had easily accessible openings along the back wall and plans for upcoming demolitions on the same street, the project team kept the site as originally constructed.

Site 3: Play Lawn

In this southwest corner of the Aetna neighborhood, flanked by sand dunes, the movable basketball hoops pulled into the quiet, limited-access residential street hinted at a demand for more active play spaces. There was little gang activity in the Aetna neighborhood, so residents were not afraid of basketball or loitering, as was the case in Cleveland. There were dilapidated basketball courts in the neighborhood, however, that made residents hesitant to request any programmed space that would require significant upkeep. Early in the design process, resident feedback gravitated toward clean, open space that would be attractive for play and socializing (figure 4-6).

Figure 4-6a. (left) A residential vacant lot on a quiet, limited-access street that abuts an electric station.

Figure 4-6b. (below) At the play lawn site in Gary, an intact driveway remnant supports a picnic table (delivered by the city on request) or games; a natural area with elevated bat houses ties the lot into the sand dunes beyond. Credit: Cooley's Video

The plan for the site was to connect the street to natural areas while providing a large play field. A designated naturalized area in the rear of the parcel provided space for eight elevated bat houses. An intact, partial driveway was preserved for placement of a picnic table; however, rather than leaving the table on site and at risk for theft, the city opted to store it centrally and deliver it upon request from the community, free of charge. Although the historical driveway apron had been demolished with the house, the curb at the street had not been replaced, so it provided an access point for street runoff flow into the rain garden—an opportunity to take advantage of existing site conditions and bypass the need for permitting to install curb cuts. At the front of the parcel, a generously sized rain garden framed the site and collected runoff from the play lawn.

Figure 4-7a. (left) A vacant lot on a street corner in Buffalo had recently benefited from the addition of a new mural and fence.

Figure 4-7b. (below) Addition of soil and plants converted the space into a public native plants garden, which provides material to other community urban greening projects.

Buffalo Project Descriptions

The West Side neighborhood of Buffalo wanted to increase their capacity to create and maintain urban green space by building an open-air plant nursery, as well as to expand existing green space through addition of a handball court and conversion of a corner vacant lot into a small park.

Site 1: Plant Nursery

In Buffalo, at a visible street corner, a new open-air plant nursery provides passive recreational space, neighborhood beautification, and habitat for birds and insects (figure 4-7). The grassy residential parcel was decorated by a colorful mural not long before it was further developed under Vacant to Vibrant. Post-installation, the parcel functions as an outdoor plant nursery for PUSH. The site is mounded with wood chips to keep weeds at bay and retain soil moisture

Figure 4-8a. (left) A large vacant parcel in Buffalo stood adjacent to a basketball court, presenting an opportunity to create a larger park.

Figure 4-8b. (below) A handball court was constructed toward the rear of the parcel. In front are picnic tables and a gently sloping lawn that directs stormwater into a rain garden.

without supplemental water. Rows of native grasses and forbs, spaced by wood chip paths, are divided and potted one or two times annually to provide plant material for other community urban greening initiatives. A split rail fence on three sides of the parcel frames it while keeping it open for visitation by community members.

At the lowest point in the parcel, a small rain garden planted in red-osier dogwood (*Cornus stolonifera*, a shrub that spreads via stolons, or underground runners) captures stormwater runoff from the rest of the parcel and from a neighboring house via a downspout disconnect. Although the rain garden is small (6 by 12 feet) and accepts runoff from a relatively large surface area (4,900 square feet), we were surprised by how quickly the soil dried out after stormwater events. The dogwood, with an open canopy that stands 6 feet tall, is capable of moving water quickly from the soil while leaving open sight lines from the sidewalk onto the parcel.

Site 2: Handball Court

Handball, a sport that involves players hitting a ball against a wall with their hands, is popular in Buffalo, so residents of the PUSH neighborhood wanted a handball court for their neighborhood (figure 4-8). This large vacant lot on Buffalo's West Side is gently sloped; prior to installation, it was a grassy area between the street and a dirt driveway leading to a basketball court in a parcel behind the lot. The new handball court sits at the high point of the parcel, at the rear. In front of the court are two picnic tables and a large lawn for sports and activities. A rain garden at the front captures runoff from a majority of the parcel.

Like all of the rain gardens and planting beds in Buffalo, and in contrast to planted areas at sites in Gary and Cleveland, the rain garden itself is simple, with only a couple varieties of flowering plants and one or two types of sedges and grasses. The PUSH maintenance crew insisted that the planting be simple to maintain a tidy appearance and to help them easily identify weeds for removal.

At this and other sites in Buffalo, the maintenance crew and designers worked uncommonly closely during the design process. Residents helped guide general site use, but the details were worked out with the maintenance crew. At times this seemed to be a mutually frustrating process, in which even the placement of a single tree was hotly debated. The end result, though, was three sites that were well within the maintenance capacity of the landscaping crew. Over time, this site and others in Buffalo have held up well, with few modifications.

Site 3: Corner Park

This project on a visible street corner was designed mostly for passive recreational use and helps provide off-street parking for an adjacent rental property (figure 4-9). Prior to installation, it was an unadorned grassy vacant lot, a mild eyesore at an intersection that received neighborhood foot and car traffic. A simple lawn was flanked on one street edge by a rain garden that ran the length of the lawn. The garden was simply decorated, containing four trees spaced between a decorative split rail fence. On the opposite side of the parcel was a parking space of pervious pavers, framed by two plant beds and a small rain garden that accepted runoff from one-half of the parcel. This site was a good illustration of how a small rain garden footprint could still have a relatively large stormwater impact—rain gardens captured runoff from the entire site, as well as from one-half of the roof area of both adjacent houses via downspout disconnections, all in a combined area of less than 200 square feet. Three years after installation, the project closely resembles the original site plans.

Figure 4-9a. (left) A small vacant parcel sat on a street corner in a mixed-use neighborhood on Buffalo's West Side.

Figure 4-9b. (below) The completed corner park adds pervious off-street parking, a bench, and a small rain garden that collects stormwater from the roofs of two adjacent houses.

Design Modifications during Installation and Maintenance

In response to circumstances that were unforeseen during project planning—such as unavailable materials, or modifications requested by contractors in response to actual site conditions, or feedback received from residents—each of the Vacant to Vibrant installations underwent varying degrees of modification after site plans were finalized. The first modifications were suggested by contractors. As they ordered materials and began preparing for installation, we heard feedback from contractors, such as "Those plants are out of stock for the season. We need to use something else" or "We tried using those rocks in another project. It was a disaster. What can we use instead?"

While the specifics of the needed modifications could not have been anticipated, many of the general reasons for modifications echoed resident feedback that first surfaced during project planning. Concerns about safety, appearance, and unintended use of projects underlay many of the changes that were made to site plans over three years of installation and maintenance.

Unavailable Materials

With plants or other design elements, unavailability sometimes resulted in minor modifications to site plans during installation. Native plants, in particular, can be limited in quantity and seasonal availability, due to difficulty in sourcing and germinating wild seeds. Designers, contractors, or suppliers were best able to identify acceptable substitutes for unavailable materials when they had a clear understanding of why the materials had been chosen in the first place. Was it more important that they match the item based on appearance or function? Any substitutions, whether plants, benches, or other features, then needed to be evaluated based on the same selection criteria that guided the original design plans—for example, suggested plant substitutes were considered based on the original plant selection criteria, outlined in chapter 3.

Maintenance Requirements

In some cases, contractors made suggested changes to design plans to decrease maintenance requirements. With this type of feedback, it was especially helpful to have the specific maintenance contractor work directly with the designer to find an acceptable compromise, although that process was sometimes frustrating for both parties and needed to be mediated by the project manager. The most common feedback was about elements that required knowledge or labor outside the capacity of the contractor. "In the spring, our crews won't be able to tell many of these plants from weeds that will be sprouting at the same time," a Cleveland maintenance contractor told us. "We need to simplify this planting." Reducing the number of plant species, choosing recognizable plants, and clumping plants by species all helped reduce the guesswork required of maintenance crews lacking experience caring for native plants, which can be hard to tell from weeds until they mature in the summer. Other reasons for plant substitutions included disease, aesthetics, and lack of survival due to climate or local conditions.

Mulched areas and aggressively spreading plants were other design elements that increased sites' maintenance requirements. Mulch degraded and needed to be replaced every one to two years. In addition, even with a barrier of landscape cloth underneath the mulch layer, weeds crept in over time. Transporting mulch—shoveling it into wheelbarrows, moving it to planting beds, dumping and spreading it to four- to six-inch depths—is hard work and may be too labor intensive for sites that are maintained by volunteer workers. Plants that must be cut back or pulled on an annual basis to control size, to preserve the health of the plant, or to remove dead material may require special expertise, heavy labor, or both, and this caused modifications to site plans over time.

Placement, numbers, and species of trees were topics of conversation around maintenance. In Buffalo, the designer proposed trees to provide vertical interest in an area where the maintenance contractor did not want trees. Because the maintenance contractor and landowner had responsibility for the site in the long term, the trees were removed from the final plans at their request. In Cleveland, the specific maintenance requirements of trees in vacant land use projects have been met with resistance by city government. Pruning trees requires specialized knowledge and equipment, and leaf pickup is labor and cost intensive. For these reasons, Vacant to Vibrant's designs largely favored shrubs, forbs, and grasses in lieu of trees. More recent research about the myriad community benefits provided by urban trees, however, including stormwater control, suggest that trees warrant stronger consideration. "Right species, right place" guidelines—that is, species selection based on site conditions—are one way that designers can include trees while being sensitive to maintenance requirements.

Placement of Features

During installation, contractors encountered conditions that required adjustments to the placement of features in design plans. Often adjustments were simple, such as altering spacing and position of elements to accommodate equipment such as mowers. Other modifications, such as adjusting the exact location of rain gardens, required closer oversight by project leaders.

While our design team tried to place rain gardens within a depression on the site where runoff would collect naturally, in practice drainage patterns sometimes differed from what was anticipated, or installation altered the direction of runoff flow. The responsibility of the landscape contractor with respect to stormwater management was to install the rain garden as closely as possible to the site plan, but also to preserve drainage patterns so that runoff would be routed to the rain garden. This was a point of needed clarification for landscape contractors: that they could, and should, prioritize function over replicating design plans exactly.

During site selection, the project team prioritized flat parcels for stormwater management. Later lessons from Vacant to Vibrant, however, demonstrated that stormwater was easier to route to rain gardens if the parcels had a slight prevailing slope. On very flat parcels, where stormwater would pool in the smallest depression, landscape contractors needed to make several fine adjustments to the local grade to ensure that runoff reached the rain garden. This involved smoothing the surface around the rain garden, filling depressions that did not link to it, and creating a drainage path to route runoff into it. With a stronger prevailing slope, minor fluctuations in grade were less important for pooling and flow of runoff.

Vandalism

Most concerns about vandalism that arose during planning had been related to gang activity; however, older youth did not cause many problems to sites in any of the three cities. One exception was the handball court in Buffalo, which was tagged with graffiti shortly after installation. (PUSH has had some success with directly asking youth leaders not to tag PUSH-owned structures and equipment.) In general, the low incidence of gang activity at urban greening sites correlates with research showing that the increased use of those sites by community members reduces their attractiveness for illicit use.

At project sites in Buffalo, community partners declined to use stones of a size small enough to be thrown but large enough to cause damage to windows, cars, and people. In Cleveland, stones were approved as part of a nature play design only after considering their potential as projectiles. We discussed a small stone "river" as part of a nature play design and, after weighing input from Buffalo, opted to try using the stones as recommended by the landscape architect and by Cleveland residents, who felt that the lessons of Buffalo were not necessarily transferable to their city. The stones were installed over geotextile landscape fabric (weed barrier). Children playing on the site displaced enough stones onto other areas of the parcel that the weed barrier was exposed in places. Subsequently, our maintenance contractor complained that stones were being thrown by lawn mowers when the grass was cut, posing a risk to the laborers maintaining the sites. Additionally, several windows of a neighboring house were broken by stones thrown by younger children. Two years after installation, the stone feature was removed due to persistent problems with stones being displaced and thrown.

Swing set chains were also frequently broken, wrapped around the top pole, or cut. Protective sheaths were added to prevent chains from being disabled, but we have subsequently heard this complaint about swing sets from collaborators in a variety of neighborhoods. In the cases of swing sets and small stones, Vacant to Vibrant would have benefited from heeding warnings from partners in Buffalo and avoided using these elements at any of our project sites. In spite of residents feeling certain that lessons from other neighborhoods were not transferable to theirs, this was an area where the experience of community leaders—even from other cities—was ultimately more accurate.

The interpretive signage manufactured for the Cleveland project had a defect in that it was possible to peel the printed layer off the wooden sign frame. After children did this, the project team worked with the sign company to adjust the construction of all signs in Cleveland, and the signs were replaced. They were peeled again, however, and were eventually removed after the manufacturer could not offer a better solution.

Other types of vandalism that were common included damage to solar lighting—a particularly attractive target for children, who seemed to enjoy climbing poles to get at the lights. In response, lights were retrofitted with protective covers, or lighting was removed. Although lighting had been among the top requests from residents during the planning phase, out of concern for safety, replacement of solar lighting after it was broken was not a high priority for residents during the maintenance phase, illustrating how direct experience with urban greening projects can influence resident concerns.

At sites in Cleveland that were designed for active play for younger children, vandalism that resulted from destructive play was a persistent problem, for which we had trouble finding a workable solution. Possible solutions include redesigning the sites to attract older visitors, who could supervise children, or dramatically reducing the complexity of the sites to remove any delicate parts. Shrubs such as sumac, which were harder to run through, proved to be more hardy in these locations compared to decorative grasses and forbs. Over time, offering children a greater variety of places to play and congregate may reduce the pressure on any one site and may alleviate some of the boredom that results in destructive play.

Dumping and Trash

Dumping on vacant lots is common in our Gary and Cleveland neighborhoods. Used automobile tires, large pieces of furniture, and construction debris—items that are a hassle or expensive to dispose of correctly—are the most commonly dumped items in these neighborhoods. Dumped materials raise the possibility of lead, asbestos, and other contaminants. To discourage dumping, we advocated removal of driveway aprons where possible and installed fences and/or flower beds along the road-facing edges of parcels to reduce the appearance of easy vehicle access. In Gary, city maintenance crews timed cleanup of a large nearby dumping site with installation of one of the Vacant to Vibrant projects. The dramatic improvement in appearance, plus the addition of bollard fencing and other barriers to keep trucks from easily accessing the site, was successful in discouraging dumping on both sites.

Trash was a notable problem on sites that were designed for active play by young children. Trash cans were added to parcels in Cleveland, first with a supply of trash bags and reliance on neighbors to place trash on the curb for weekly pickup. (We worked with the city to have these sites added to the municipal trash collection route but were not successful.) In Buffalo and Gary, maintenance crews assumed responsibility for trash cans that were placed on site.

Downspout Disconnections and Curb Cuts

In green infrastructure projects, which continue to be novel and experimental in many locations, designs often bump up against the limited ability of local agencies to work outside their existing policies and comfort zones. At the time of Vacant to Vibrant implementation, Cleveland and Gary had existing examples of rain gardens as green infrastructure, but neither had yet had much experience with projects that diverted runoff from streets and buildings into stormwater control measures. As such, these cities lacked policies that governed widespread use of curb cuts and downspout disconnections. Successful implementation of such measures in these cities relied on taking advantage of existing conditions and working within the confines of existing regulations. In some cases, though, we had to discard these elements of design plans and be satisfied with stormwater control of site runoff only.

The original Vacant to Vibrant design plans incorporated a downspout disconnection in every location where there was an immediately adjacent house. (We excluded houses that were separated from the parcel by a driveway to avoid the cost of tunneling under existing impervious surface, given our modest project budget.) In the end, we were able to incorporate downspout disconnections in only two sites in Buffalo.

City officials in Cleveland and Gary ultimately declined to approve plans for downspout disconnections, due to lack of an official city ordinance or policy regarding disconnection of downspouts from the combined sewer system, as well as concerns about routing stormwater from privately owned parcels onto city-owned parcels, which sparked questions about long-term liability and maintenance.

Although Buffalo did not have an official policy about downspout disconnections, landownership in Buffalo was clearer—in both cases, PUSH owned the vacant parcel and the adjacent house as part of its rental program. Thus, downspout disconnections to route stormwater from impervious surfaces onto vacant parcels were easiest to pursue in cases where ownership was consistent between parcels, which clarified questions of liability, maintenance, and ownership. For future projects involving downspout disconnections onto vacant parcels, in the absence of clear policy about instances of multiple ownership, our project team will pursue projects where multiple parcels have a single owner.

Likewise, Vacant to Vibrant design plans added curb cuts to divert street runoff into rain gardens when existing slopes were suitable for runoff flow. Curb cuts were planned for four of the nine parcels, two each in Gary and Cleveland. In Cleveland, a feature of the local neighborhood was that the curbs separating the road from the grassy strip adjacent to the street (locally termed the "tree lawn") were only an inch high or, at some points, flush with the street. In these locations, installation of rain gardens that functioned as curb cuts in the right-of-way did not require permits—it was allowed under normal landscaping regulations, because it did not involve altering the curb and did not connect to the sewer system. Taking advantage of existing conditions allowed us to bypass a lengthy permitting process (6–12 months) in these instances. Rain gardens in the right-of-way that were planted with grasses and forbs were quickly trampled by foot and vehicle traffic, however. Plants in right-of-way rain gardens were later replaced with lawn seed, which obscured the obvious stormwater management purpose but did not affect the underlying functionality of stormwater capture.

In Gary, a rain garden was installed in a former driveway apron, where no curb existed—a permit was not needed there either. In a second location in Gary, we talked with the stormwater/sewer authority within city government about inspecting the curb and permitting actual cuts that would connect rain gardens to the street. The city declined to issue permits for cuts to be made, citing concerns that cuts would pose a risk to cars that might clip the curb cuts while driving. With design modifications and additional municipal examples of curb cuts in Gary, it may have been possible to work through these concerns; however, we chose not to pursue curb cuts in this location due to time constraints.

Resident Complaints

In spite of extensive community engagement during the planning phase, there were aspects of projects that dissatisfied residents after installation. We received complaints about the way project sites were being used by community members and about the sites' appearance. Community engagement to address resident complaints during this phase of the project involved a different group of residents than during the planning phase. These complaints tended to come mostly from residents who lived very close to the sites—usually adjacent or across the street. Some of these residents had not been involved in community engagement during the planning phase, either by choice or by circumstance. Other complaints came from extended family members—often adult children of older residents—who lived elsewhere but spent a lot of time near the sites.

Parks that facilitated more active recreation, like those with play equipment for small children, attracted the most complaints about noise and trash. Similarly, there were complaints about mischief created by young children, such as climbing fences, and about play spilling over into the yards of adjacent homeowners. At one of the two project sites in Cleveland with a swing set, the adult daughter of an elderly neighbor frequently complained about the noise created by children next door. Sometimes the children would climb her mother's fence, or hop the fence entirely to run through the backyard. By way of remedy, she requested that the lot return to being vacant, arguing that a vacant lot would at least be quieter.

When we talked with the mother directly, however, offering to build a better fence, she insisted that the children were not a nuisance and that the site was not bad. (From talking with community leaders who knew the family, we surmised that the truth was probably somewhere in between. The mother was hard of hearing, so she was less sensitive to noise, but the kids who wandered away from the site's swing set were definitely causing mischief on her property.) In this case, we were caught between the mother and the daughter. The daughter insisted on a better fence, but the mother—the homeowner—refused when we asked permission to build it. In the end, a fence was not built, and the complaints subsided over time.

Regarding the sites' appearance, there were typically complaints if the grass got too tall between mowings. At sites designed to have a more natural look, which use low-mow lawns and tall, flowering prairie plants, such complaints are common. In two instances, complaints escalated to the removal of plants from rain gardens by residents. In the one case in which we were able to identify and interview a man who had removed plants from a rain garden near the front of the walled garden site in Gary, the reason he gave was that there were "too many" plants. (He had also complained about connectivity in the rear of the parcel and had not been involved in the earlier community planning efforts.)

At the active play site in Cleveland, after installation had been completed in the fall, we arrived one day to find that the taller native plants from the rain garden had been uprooted and stacked neatly at the back of the parcel (box 4-1). Blue nitrile gloves were discarded in the grass near the plants. We were unable to find the person responsible and so cannot be sure of the reason. Given the location and other kinds of feedback we had heard in the neighborhood, though, it was likely that the person did not like the appearance of the plants, or was worried about the plants in relation to children on the site, possibly as a safety hazard.

In other cases, complaints about the appearance of project sites were more serious, straining trust that we had built in the community and requiring intervention by the project team. In Cleveland, we made major overhauls to the nature play installation after sustained negative feedback from residents that continued after implementation. Residents were unhappy with the appearance of the site, both due to original design components that did not translate well from renderings to real life, and to problems that arose during maintenance. After installation, the play log and tire benches that had blended into site design plans ended up being prominent visual features in the built site. Their close resemblance to the fallen trees and dumped tires that dotted the neighborhood could not be overlooked; they were subsequently removed. In a similar vein, the grassy play mounds that were built on the site proved

---

Box 4-1. Email about plant removal

> **Date:** October 30, 2015 at 4:44:26 PM EDT
> **From:** Ryan Mackin
> **To:** Sandra Albro
> **Subject:** sites update

Crestwood: Unfortunately someone(s) took it up themself to unearth all the plants at the back of the site—both beyond the zigzag fence and in the rain garden. Photos of the "fun game" are attached. As you see, plants were piled up nicely in the back and the rain garden is now plantless—although it wasn't looking too good this summer anyhow. I'm guessing it was neighborhood kids who did it, although I found used rubber gloves out back, which could indicate adult involvement if that's what the gloves were used for. Also, the "neatness" of the effort seems suspect, but I guess it's safer to default that it was just the kids.

to be an eyesore over time and were eventually removed. They were difficult to mow and dried out more quickly than flat ground; after a particularly hot and dry summer, the grass that had been planted on them died, and over time, prominent spots of bare soil filled with urban weeds. Whether covered with grass or not, they recalled the mounds and pits common to older house demolitions that had taken place prior to ordinances requiring removal of debris from the site and a level finished grade. In the end, the soil mounds were removed and the overall site grade was leveled.

A final element of the nature play site that was amended was the stone swale that formed a dry riverbed around the play mounds. Children were fond of throwing the round river-washed gravel, which had resulted in dented cars and several broken windows in the house bordering the site. This was consistent with the experience of Buffalo and the Northeast Ohio Regional Sewer District that using anything but very fine stone or large boulders as decorative features in urban greening projects was unwise. The project team purchased replacement window glass for the neighboring house and replaced the river rock with mulch; later the mulch swale was amended again, this time to lawn to reduce weeds.

Another round of community engagement was initiated to identify a replacement element for the stone swale. By that time, we had the benefit of feedback about the other Cleveland Vacant to Vibrant site with a swing set—it had generated numerous noise complaints from neighbors, and the chains had already needed to be replaced once. This was consistent with feedback we had received from Buffalo and from Cleveland Metroparks, both of which had stopped installing swing sets on their own properties. We encouraged the block club to consider other options, but they were adamant in wanting a swing set for kids. Seeking to soothe the hurt feelings evoked by the original project design, we agreed. Over time, however, the swing set proved to have similar problems to the one on Crestwood; children or others repeatedly wrapped the swings around the top pole and broke or cut the chains, rendering them useless until they could be fixed. Thus the swings were inoperable a lot of the time.

In the end, the amended project remained as a swing set, park bench, and bioretention area on a grassy lot—simple and functional, but not as transformative as the original design had envisioned (figure 4-10).

Inclusivity

After installation, we recognized that two sites in Gary were not ADA accessible[1] due to use of crushed rock for pathways. An advantage of crushed rock is that it is pervious to stormwater runoff; however, the rocks were loose enough to make it difficult to push a wheelchair or stroller. We looked into the use of polymers or other means

Figure 4-10. The nature play site in Cleveland was later amended to include a swing set and traditional park benches, replacing the play log and tire benches.

to stabilize the rock, but after investigating options, we did not find one that would have been reasonably priced to purchase and retrofit. After considering cost options, the city of Gary made the decision to leave the sites as is but to commit to ADA-compliant walkways for future urban greening projects.

ADA compliance had not been considered for parcels in Cleveland either. On parcels with swing sets, ADA-compliant walkways, at least from sidewalk to park benches, would have made it easier for older residents to supervise young children who lived with them or came to visit. ADA accessibility, in general, is frequently overlooked in vacant land use projects and stormwater management features. In these projects, pervious pavement is one option for paths that would increase accessibility to residents while meeting other project goals for stormwater control and sustainability.

Plant Nurseries
In many cities, it is difficult to find a reliable, affordable source of plant material that is well suited to urban greening installations. Native plants and other specialized plant material are offered by only a few growers regionally, due to the difficulty of sourcing and germinating seeds. In organizations that construct or maintain a large number of urban greening projects, or in cities where such entities exist, constructing a plant nursery can help address problems of affordability and supply.

In places where local sources of native and other plants appropriate for sustainable urban greening projects do not exist, we consider building urban plant nurseries to be an important part of growing local capacity for taking practical, affordable urban greening to scale. Plant nurseries can also help preserve local genetic material, an important aspect of biodiversity. Capital costs for a nursery can be easily justified—the construction costs of up to $14,000 per nursery were roughly equal to the cost of plant material for the three Vacant to Vibrant projects built in the same community. Cost is often not the biggest limiting factor, however; plant nurseries require knowledgeable growers, who are still in short supply.

PUSH was fortunate to have an experienced plant grower on staff, which greatly simplified the process of designing and building a nursery in Buffalo. Their plant nursery can serve as a template that can be used elsewhere. In addition to the open-air plant nursery that formed part of one of the Buffalo Vacant to Vibrant project sites, PUSH used a separate, paved vacant parcel in the neighborhood as a site for the construction of a large polyurethane hoop house ($4,000, from a kit), part of a multilayer hoop house system that was influenced by Will Allen's Growing Power in Milwaukee (see figure 5-2).[2] Covered gutters that divert runoff from the side of the hoop house collect rain and snowmelt into external cisterns that provide ample water for growing plants year-round; the addition of duckweed and minnows to internal water storage tanks keeps mosquito larvae from growing in stagnant water. Twice per week, a battery-operated pump moves water from the storage tanks to floodable grow tables to water containers of plants. (An alternative system could use soaker hoses to pump harvested water throughout the hoop house using grid or solar power.) Under the grow tables are vermiculture composting bins—a source of organic material for plants, and a modest heat source for the hoop house in winter months—as well as mats of burlap sacks that are used to cultivate oyster mushrooms. During planting of rain gardens and beds, these burlap sacks are spread between soil and mulch layers to inoculate plants with fungal mycelia that aid in plant establishment.

Beyond serving as an ecologically sustainable source of affordable plant material, the plant nursery allows PUSH to have control over the species and cultivars that it uses for its urban greening projects. The plant nursery can also be a source of revenue by selling plants, if desired. The hoop house works in tandem with an open-air plant nursery built as one of Buffalo's Vacant to Vibrant projects—while the open-air plant nursery takes advantage of local climate conditions to reduce the effort needed to grow plants, it is possible to split plants for transplanting into other locations only in the spring or fall. In contrast, the hoop house provides containerized plants that are easy to move and can be transplanted throughout the growing season.

In Gary, city government did not have staff with nursery-growing experience—a common scenario in government park maintenance departments. Although we had funding in Gary to support construction of a plant nursery, we were limited by the ability of project partners to maintain and utilize it. Toward the end of the project timeline, a church in the nearby neighborhood of Emerson began development of an urban farming educational program for youth. We were able to partner with this church to help them expand their program, with the agreement that a portion of their plant material would be used to support Vacant to Vibrant and other community greening projects.

In Cleveland, we were ultimately unable to find a project partner or local community group with the capacity to undertake an urban plant nursery within the timeline of the project. Early in the project, the nursery was part of a planned expansion of the Cleveland Botanical Garden's Green Corps urban farming educational program. Plans for the expansion changed after the botanical garden's integration with Holden Arboretum to form Holden Forests & Gardens. Other community groups in Cleveland did not have the in-house expertise to support a plant nursery.

The business model of a plant-growing operation is different in Cleveland too; urban greening projects there continue to be splintered among many different organizations and branches of local government, few of whom are purchasing plants at a level that would justify growing them themselves. In addition, Cleveland benefits from having a healthy plant nursery industry within a one-hour drive of the city.

In 2018, a few community organizations in Cleveland are talking with each other about constructing an urban plant nursery. Given ongoing regional conversations about climate resilience, vacant land use, sustainability, and urban tree canopy, it is likely that one will be built in the future.

Lessons Learned from Implementation

Community engagement lessons from the project planning phase (described in chapter 3) continued to be instructive for the Vacant to Vibrant project team through implementation and project maintenance. Residents were helpful sources of information about potential problems that could interfere with the social benefits of urban greening projects and that would reduce their value for neighborhood stabilization. One example of how residents' help was beneficial may be seen in the absence in large measure, at the nine Vacant to Vibrant sites, of a potential problem that consumed much energy during planning: older youth using the sites for drugs, gambling, and other unwanted activities. Resident advice about programming and design that would discourage such use allowed us to create nine project sites where this problem did not surface in a significant way.

There were limits to residents' understanding, however, as shown by the swing sets that residents overwhelmingly supported for two Cleveland sites, in spite of cautions from community partners in other cities that ultimately proved justified. As residents learn about urban greening alongside practitioners, particularly in neighborhoods that have not seen much recent investment, it can be helpful to supplement resident knowledge with lessons learned from other locations. Lessons from Buffalo, where the West Side has seen a number of vacant land reuse projects, were instructive in Cleveland and Gary. In addition, community liaisons can help practitioners balance resident knowledge of their own neighborhoods with information from outside.

Two lessons highlight potential conflicts between different types of vacant land reuse strategies that might be layered into one project, as in Vacant to Vibrant. First, projects that supported very active play were frequent sources of neighbor complaints and maintenance problems. One exception, the handball court that was successful in Buffalo, occupied the rear of a very large vacant parcel, with clear separation from stormwater management, and abutted a lot with an existing basketball court. In the small confines of a normal vacant residential lot, passive recreation may be a more appropriate land use in close proximity to stormwater control measures and neighboring homes.

Secondly, there may be inherent conflict between urban greening that is designed for neighborhood stabilization and green infrastructure that is meant for stormwater control. Community engagement processes try to instill a sense of ownership of urban greening projects among residents, to foster stewardship, maintenance, and advocacy for projects. When vacant lots become part of a neighborhood's stormwater infrastructure, however, responsibility for stormwater function is held by a landowner or sewer/stormwater authority, more akin to power or road infrastructure. Conflicts can arise when, as in Vacant to Vibrant, residents interfere with rain gardens because they do not see or support their purpose in taking up space in their community. These conflicts can be minimized by adapting green infrastructure to the preferences of the community's residents and by community engagement that emphasizes shared ownership.

Absence of continuity in project partners is a threat to the implementation of urban greening projects that can be reduced through formal agreements that clearly outline the responsibility of parties, the project timeline, and expected communication. Even the process of creating an agreement is useful for identifying multiple points of contact within an organization and ensuring that the organization's leadership is on board with the partnership. Our written agreements with project partners in Vacant to Vibrant were never put to legal challenge but proved helpful for clearly communicating the terms of project partnerships, on which either party could lean for added support when needed.

Finally, as practitioners continue to create best practices for urban greening projects, the added uncertainty of such projects suggests that a higher-than-usual allocation of project budget to contingency funding would be wise. Often, landscape contractors recommend 10 percent of a project budget for contingency funding to cover unforeseen circumstances. Modifications to Vacant to Vibrant projects—though optional and considered an important part of the learning process for this initiative—ranged up to 50 percent for the nature play installation. For the other eight projects, a 20 percent contingency would have been adequate to cover unforeseen problems, such as diseased tree removal and (in Cleveland) parcel boundary surveys, and to protect against many additional risks. This recommended amount of contingency is itself contingent upon allowing a lengthy process for parcel selection, which was an important element in decreasing the risk of common problems in vacant lots, such as underground storage tanks or buried building debris, that require costly remediation or relocation.

5

Sustaining Urban Greening Projects

Maintenance of urban greening projects goes beyond physically caring for sites. It involves building local knowledge about how to care for projects, putting systems in place to support green space—building policy, creating a workforce—and changing expectations about what urban green space should look like. These changes require multidirectional vision that recognizes the past processes that created vacant land and infrastructure problems, sees the present issues of physical maintenance requirements and community needs for stabilization, and looks forward to changes that will be necessary to support building healthier, resilient neighborhoods.

Building equitable urban green infrastructure will require moving past pilot projects to establishing best practices that streamline decision making. In turn, these best practices need a firm foundation that is built on solid assumptions. In this chapter, we will revisit maintenance requirements of urban greening projects like Vacant to Vibrant. We will discuss examples of how communities are building maintenance capacity and explore additional considerations, beyond the physical upkeep of sites, that are necessary for building community goodwill and trust in urban greening practices.

Green Infrastructure Professional Networks

In early stages of green infrastructure implementation, it can be difficult to identify potential green infrastructure project partners, because the types of partnering organizations and job titles of individuals who are essential for green infrastructure projects vary widely among cities. This complicates replication of green infrastructure practices among communities. The functional roles that are needed from project partners in an urban greening project are more standardized, however, so it can be useful to start with the list of roles that need to be filled and then work backward to identify the person(s) who might fill each role in a given community:

- Designer (for aesthetic elements)
- Engineer (for technical elements)
- Plant materials source
- Soil source
- Hardscape source
- Permit approval
- Community liaison for resident engagement
- Community liaison for process
- Landowner for purchase or lease
- Installation contractor
- Maintenance contractor
- Project manager

The types of organizations, and the titles of the people working there, differed among the three Vacant to Vibrant cities. In a small city such as Gary, where there were fewer unique partners, one partner filled several roles—for example, one or two people within the City of Gary Department of Green Urbanism assisted as community liaison, landowner, and permit approver. In Buffalo, we chose the West Side neighborhood because of the strong organization there that was already acting in multiple capacities and could fill multiple partnering roles, which proved to be helpful for the project leaders, who did not have an existing presence in Buffalo and were unlikely to establish one long term. One downside to high levels of redundancy within the partner network, though, is that it makes the network less robust to personnel changes. And although it was not our experience, if we had had no choice but to implement our project within a specific small community, a small partnering network would have been difficult to work with if there were people within it who were not interested in, or who were opposed to, what we wanted to do. In contrast, although the logistics of working with more partners are more complicated, the benefit of a larger partner network, like the urban greening network in Cleveland, is that there are often several options for partners to fill each role, so there are more redundancies and fewer gatekeepers that can make or break a project.

In collaboration with researchers at the University of Montana, we set out to examine whether it was possible to map a specific urban greening network—the green stormwater infrastructure professional network in Cleveland—as a first step toward understanding features of professional networks that could promote success of urban greening projects across different communities.[1] We created a list of professionals within the Cleveland green stormwater infrastructure network, starting with known contacts and then asking those contacts for recommendations for additional contacts (a method that is helpful for capturing individuals within a network who may otherwise be hard to identify, due to a small number of network connections). Next we surveyed members to examine how individuals influenced others within the professional network—the type of knowledge each person had, how and with whom they shared it, and their personal attitudes (commitment, satisfaction) toward green stormwater infrastructure (figure 5-1). In total, we surveyed 28 members (80 percent) of the Cleveland professional network who worked on various aspects of green infrastructure as employees of universities, government, contractors, or community and environmental organizations. By looking at connections among individuals in the network, we found that professionals who were regarded by others as leaders in Cleveland green infrastructure tended to have more collaborative partnerships, worked more frequently with others in the network, were more central to the network (a measure of importance), and were more trusted by their peers to be competent and to operate with goodwill. Interestingly, and in contrast to many business professional networks, informal leaders among Cleveland green infrastructure professionals were more likely to be women.

Establishing open, collaborative, resilient networks takes time, care, and trust. Agreements among professionals in the network, whether formal agreements as discussed in chapter 4, or a set of bylaws or shared goals that may be articulated as part of establishing an alliance, can be helpful for navigating tensions that are likely to arise within networks around competition for funding, recognition, and ownership. The survey of the Cleveland green infrastructure network provides a useful snapshot about collaborations that affect green stormwater infrastructure implementation in one city. Similar studies in other cities—an area for future work—could help characterize professional networks that create successful urban greening projects. By mapping several cities' networks, perhaps it would be possible to develop prescriptive guidelines for how urban greening networks should be developed, so that they are robust and effective enough to create lasting change.

Figure 5-1. Community liaisons and landscapers that support green infrastructure projects in Cleveland and Buffalo learn about infiltration in a Vacant to Vibrant workshop.

What Constitutes "Low Maintenance"?

With implementation of projects that were designed to be low maintenance, we were reminded that there is no absolute measure of low maintenance—maintenance burden is judged in relation to available capacity. Some aspects of the Vacant to Vibrant sites had low labor requirements for mowing, mulching, or watering but required specialized knowledge for installation and care, such as trees. Other aspects of our projects did not require specialized knowledge and were low maintenance for able-bodied crews of laborers, but proved too labor intensive for volunteer laborers; mulching fell into this category. Lastly, some types of maintenance fell outside the skills or interests of landscaping crews. On sites that attracted a lot of use (particularly by young children), trash that was scattered through lawn pickup increased the effort and cost of mowing, while swing set chains needed frequent repair and unwinding. These were common sources of complaints from landscape contractors and residents alike.

To identify whether sites fit available maintenance capacity, we considered the specific skill sets of our landscape contractors and, for best results, enlisted their help during the planning process to make sure we ended up with projects that matched their knowledge, ability, and scope of work (table 5-1). In general, simplifying project designs—reducing the number of design elements and plant species, and more clearly separating land uses within project sites—helped reduce maintenance requirements. The trade-off for simplification is that project sites may have had less visual impact in the period immediately following installation. However, over time, maintenance capacity had the largest effect on site appearance and resident satisfaction. Simpler projects tended to remain the most tidy, had the fewest complaints from maintenance contractors and residents, and required the fewest labor hours to maintain.

Table 5-1. Vacant to Vibrant seasonal site maintenance tasks per neighborhood*

Month	Labor Hours	Maintenance Tasks
April (spring cleanup)	6	Remove trash and debris Mow and trim lawn Prune woody plants Check and repair equipment
May	8	Remove trash and debris Mow and trim lawn Weed and mulch beds Weed paths and hard surfaces
June	8	Remove trash and debris Mow and trim lawn Weed beds Add new plants to beds
July	4	Remove trash and debris Mow and trim lawn Water new plants
August	6	Remove trash and debris Mow and trim lawn Water new plants Mow natural areas (once per year)
September	4	Remove trash and debris Mow and trim lawn Over-seed lawn
October (fall cleanup)	8	Remove trash and debris Mow and trim lawn Cut decorative grasses (optional) Plant trees Check and repair equipment

*Labor hours are aggregated for 3 sites/1 neighborhood.

Projects that encouraged active play and were targeted toward younger children had higher maintenance requirements. In Cleveland, vandalism proved to be an intractable problem at active-play sites, where children could find entertainment in destructive play as well as in interacting with the play equipment as intended. One day, while working on site with the maintenance contractor, we watched a young girl about nine years old push a shopping cart from an adjacent lot, roll it under the swing set, balance inside of the cart so she could reach, and then methodically wrap the chains of both swings around the top crossbar of the swing set. We approached and talked with her, explaining that the swings could not be used by kids that way and asking her to unwind them. She shrugged, slowly unwound the swings until they draped over each side of the shopping cart, and left. On a quiet residential day with no other kids in sight and no adults nearby, she had found a way to pass some time. On a separate occasion, young children proudly showed us how they could scale the light poles and disassemble or break off the solar lights. Over time, the layout of active-play sites in Cleveland was simplified to reduce maintenance requirements by reducing the number of components that could be repeatedly broken.

Native Plants and Green Infrastructure

Native plants are a very common feature of rain gardens; as such, green stormwater infrastructure has become closely associated with native plants. We are concerned, however, that an automatic pairing poses a risk to widespread adoption of both green infrastructure and native plantings. Common complaints associated with the appearance and maintenance of green infrastructure often have less to do with its functionality than with the burden of planting and caring for the native plants that are commonly used in it. Although native species of grasses and forbs are easy to grow in theory, requiring little supplemental water or nutrients once established, there is a learning curve to proper care that, if not followed, can result in failed plants, wasted funds, and hard feelings. This goes both ways—negative experiences with green stormwater infrastructure can bias land managers away from native plants, even while there are urban vacant areas where native plantings constitute a high-priority land use.

Green infrastructure projects that include native plants should consider seasonal requirements for germination and planting that affect their availability (and increase their cost). For vacant lot projects paired with house demolition that can take place at any time of year, seasonal restrictions on plant availability can pose a problem. Temporary solutions that can tide projects over until planting windows in spring and fall include erosion cloth and/or a temporary groundcover.

Once established, native plants do not have intense maintenance requirements for pruning, watering, or nutrients, but they do require specialized maintenance for which traditional landscape contractors are often unprepared. Most native grasses and forbs die down in the fall and re-emerge in the spring. As mentioned previously, untrained eyes have difficulty discerning spring shoots from undesired native and nonnative plants. For this reason, experienced green infrastructure maintainers, such as our project partners at People United for Sustainable Housing (PUSH), advocate for simplification of native plantings to a very small number of species, as well as grouping species into clumps or rows, so it is easy for maintenance crews to learn to discern wanted plants from unwanted ones.

A final consideration for native plants in urban green infrastructure projects, frequently heard from both maintenance contractors and residents, is about the aesthetics of the plants. Native plants are still considered foreign in urban settings; they are tall (many native forbs and grasses are indigenous to tall grass prairies and approach six feet in height); and they have not gone through extensive artificial selection by horticulturists for beauty—that is, to many residents, they look like weeds. Humans untrained in ecology associate weeds with a host of undesirable things, such as vermin and neighborhood disinvestment. Thus, looking like weeds accounts for perhaps the biggest risk for native plantings—that they may be mown or uprooted by humans who do not want them in their communities, as frequently happens. Given the cost of native plants, human intervention can easily account for thousands of dollars of lost investment.

That said, native plants contribute numerous proven benefits to urban areas. They provide food and habitat for native insects, birds, and animals, which are increasingly threatened by urbanization and climate change. Cities on the Great Lakes, such as Cleveland, are important stopovers for migrating insects and birds looking for a rest stop before and after crossing large expanses of open water. Native plantings are crucial oases for animals within harsh urban landscapes.

More careful consideration of native plants should include discussions about responsible use of cultivars ("nativars") and local plant genotypes. If a main goal of an urban greening project is incorporating native plants into rain gardens to provide food and habitat to insects and animals, then the source of native plant stock should be carefully considered; as much as possible, natives should be sourced from local growers who collect local seed stock. If that is not practicable or possible in a location, or if natives are desired only for their low-maintenance properties, then it may be worth reconsidering whether nativars, nonlocal natives, and nonnative plants that are more attractive to humans and easier to cultivate in a highly urban setting would work as well, weighed against the possible ecological impacts of such decisions.

As opposed to automatically pairing native plants and green infrastructure, can these two land uses be decoupled to allow for advocacy of both, where and when they are best suited? Such advocacy may serve each cause better in the long run by limiting the number of bad experiences that the general public has with them. A broader array of landscaping options for green infrastructure is available than is often presented, because current research assumes that the plants adorning rain gardens and bioswales have no effect on stormwater control. (We suspect that future research will show that plants have a larger effect on green infrastructure performance than previously assumed—more on this in the next chapter.) Thus, in areas where native plants do not fit with the aesthetic preferences of land managers or residents, green infrastructure can be planted with turf grass, trees, or ornamental plants that are customized to community preferences for appearance and maintenance requirements. When, in the future, aesthetic preferences for a site have shifted, stormwater management areas can be reconfigured to include natives.

Maintenance and Green Workforce Development

Green workforce demands are expected to increase as cities move toward more sustainable practices; this workforce will be built from existing, adapted, and new occupations that relate to different aspects of sustainability.[2] Investment in green workforce development is also an opportunity to build social equity by providing training opportunities and job access to underserved populations.[3]

In Vacant to Vibrant cities, community organizations and municipal government partners model how such programs can help build equity. Three examples from Vacant to Vibrant project team members show how different methods can work for different locations: in Buffalo, a nonprofit organization is testing a spin-off social business enterprise; in Gary, municipal government is building green infrastructure skills into their parks maintenance department; and in Cleveland, local philanthropy is supporting entrepreneurship in sustainable landscaping.

Buffalo: Green Infrastructure Social Enterprise Business

To address shortages in skilled workers who can install and maintain green infrastructure and other new sustainable land use practices, as well as to address a shortage of "high-road"[4] employment options for residents in their neighborhood, PUSH in Buffalo began building and training their own green workforce. In 2012, PUSH formed a social enterprise landscaping business, PUSH Blue, to add an environmental justice and community-focused lens to Buffalo's combined sewer overflow problem and ensure that multiple benefits of this work would be felt in impacted communities.

Sourcing adult workers from their neighborhood on Buffalo's West Side, PUSH Blue employs a small crew of people who learn to install and manage PUSH's vacant land and home weatherization projects. PUSH Blue leverages the job-creating power of local drivers of green infrastructure, including the Buffalo Sewer Authority's commitment to green infrastructure and long-term control plan with the US Environmental Protection Agency, as well as recent changes by the City of Buffalo to its zoning code that allow for green infrastructure.

The PUSH Blue social enterprise landscaping business strives to balance competitive bidding with fair, livable wages, high-quality work, and experiences that provide quality career options for their workers. PUSH Blue hires and trains local residents for green infrastructure work as well as for green jobs, including energy efficiency retrofit work. Training includes OSHA 10 and on-the-ground experience through multiple projects, such as green stormwater infrastructure (including rain gardens, bioswales, rainwater harvesting from homes and buildings, living roofs, and permeable parking pads), urban gardens, street tree planting, bioremediation, habitat restoration, and green infrastructure maintenance. In 2015, PUSH Blue negotiated a contract with the Buffalo Sewer Authority to install green infrastructure treatments on 221 demolition sites over a two-year period, testing whether its social enterprise model could provide clients with expertise, experience, and the social benefits of high-road job creation. In total, the contract improved 19 acres of vacant land, created 53 jobs (a majority of which were held by residents of Buffalo and people of color), and provided training and technical assistance to other contractors. It has been subsequently highlighted as a regional model for equitable water management.[5]

PUSH Blue also partners with the Buffalo Sewer Authority and other local groups on a citywide downspout disconnection program, and it contracts with state agencies, public schools, and private companies to install and maintain green infrastructure. The plant nursery built as part of Vacant to Vibrant supplies PUSH with native and locally grown plants for its projects and for sale to other urban greening initiatives (figure 5-2).

Ongoing challenges to PUSH Blue's business model include finding appropriate certification programs; balancing those with on-the-ground training; and balancing job creation with the real-life limitations faced by some workers, such as not having a driver's license. On the maintenance side of projects, PUSH is refining how to budget and pay for maintenance of sites that are often installed with grant or capital funds, matching site design with actual maintenance capacity, and choosing good materials that match individual site conditions and microclimates, while also surviving the typical challenges of urban environments, such as high-traffic environments, sudden inundation of rain, and drought.

Figure 5-2. A new hoop house adds plant growing and storage space to a paved vacant lot in Buffalo. Stormwater collected from the roof waters plants that will be used for community urban greening projects.

Gary: Municipal Park Maintenance That Is Green-Infrastructure Savvy

When the Vacant to Vibrant initiative began, the City of Gary lacked a park maintenance crew. In 2012, it formed an Urban Conservation Team consisting of nine employees and residents of Gary. The city began training this crew not only to manage programmed green space, such as parks, but also to undertake maintenance of numerous green infrastructure projects that were being built in the city. These projects resulted from several successful grant requests from the City of Gary to support green stormwater infrastructure to address the city's consent decree for combined sewer overflows, and for economic revitalization that the city was engaging in around sustainability.

At the time of the Vacant to Vibrant project installation, the Urban Conservation Team had not had sufficient experience with green stormwater infrastructure to complete the installation. We were able to require the installation contractor to use the Urban Conservation Team for any cleanup or site preparation, however, as well as to provide the team with access to sites during installation so that they could observe and learn from the installation process. As the maintenance contractor, the team benefited from this hands-on opportunity to learn about the maintenance requirements of sites, including the setup and intended purpose of all of the installation components. Close cooperation between the installation and maintenance contractors also benefited the Vacant to Vibrant initiative by ensuring continuity in site appearance and function over time.

Subsequently, the Urban Conservation Team has gained enough expertise to take over installation of some new green stormwater projects. In addition, maintenance of the Vacant to Vibrant sites has avoided some of the problems encountered in Cleveland due to discontinuity of maintenance contractors, and the sites have continued to avoid problems encountered in other vacant lots in Gary, such as dumping.

Cleveland: Supporting Entrepreneurship with Green Infrastructure Maintenance

In Cleveland, plans for Vacant to Vibrant had integrated maintenance of the projects into an expansion of the Cleveland Botanical Garden's work-study program in urban agriculture for youth, Green Corps. In 2010, the botanical garden was considering expanding Green Corps to provide broader work experience that would prepare students for a variety of green jobs in landscape maintenance, sustainability, and environmental science. Vacant to Vibrant installations would have given students direct experience in new sustainability methods that many landscape professionals were looking to build their expertise in. In 2014, however, plans to expand Green Corps were put on hold following changes in institutional leadership.

Spurred by the declining quality of the installations under volunteer maintenance—fine for mowing but insufficient as a long-term, comprehensive plan—a local community foundation underwrote ongoing support for Vacant to Vibrant project maintenance. This allowed the project team to work with local community groups to identify a neighborhood-based entrepreneur who was building a landscaping company in the area, who agreed to take on maintenance of the three project sites. Through modifying plantings to fit his crew's capacity for maintenance and providing him with continuing education in sustainability topics, we helped expand the portfolio and knowledge base of his small enterprise to include principles of green stormwater infrastructure.

This arrangement highlights a vulnerability that Vacant to Vibrant shares with many vacant lot projects. Given that such projects are often installed using a one-time funding source, if the original maintenance plan falls through and funding to support maintenance is lost, what happens to the sites? This vulnerability is particularly severe for parcels that are owned by a third party. In this case, the City of

Cleveland owns the parcels, and low development pressure in the area means they will likely remain vacant for the foreseeable future. The city does not have the capacity to maintain the lots in their current state—their maintenance program is built around mowing lots with a tractor and flail mower. Their crews of lawnmowers and weed eaters are already overwhelmed by the thousands of vacant lots in their land bank, so they have no ability to care for small parks.

In the event of a loss of funding for ongoing maintenance, the Vacant to Vibrant installations in Cleveland have two options. The site designs could be further scaled back so that the sites could be mown by city maintenance crews. This would result in loss of much of the plant material in converting parcels back to lawn that could be quickly mown seven times per year. Several of the amenities would also have to be removed to accommodate city mowers—either in an official way, through deinstallation by the city or the project team, or in an unofficial way, through vandalism, scrapping, or community cleanup. Alternatively, site maintenance could perhaps be folded into another community program. At the time of publication, the project team was in conversation with a local church that was interested in incorporating the Vacant to Vibrant sites into a growing neighborhood stewardship program. If neither option proves possible, these sites would face the same fate as other small parks in the area—they would fall back into disrepair and disuse.

In contrast to the more successful maintenance in Gary and Buffalo, where the owners of the parcels have undertaken this responsibility, who conducts maintenance on a leased parcel is less certain. Given this experience and the risk that the sites may be lost in the future, and the damage that would do to a community which has already endured decades of decline, it is clear that the ideal scenario is for the liability for urban greening projects to be assumed from the beginning by the landowner, who is responsible for their long-term upkeep.

Green Infrastructure in Changing Neighborhoods

As urban greening projects remedy some neighborhood problems, they often create new ones. Even well-maintained projects can provoke worries among residents about changes that are in store for the community. Understanding the histories of post-industrial neighborhoods—how they were developed, including the types of residents who have historically benefited from development and those who have been excluded (see chapter 2)—in addition to keeping community dialogue open and utilizing community liaisons, can help urban greening professionals sensitively navigate resident concerns about change.

How Experience with Urban Greening Shapes Expectations

The Gary and Cleveland neighborhoods differed from Buffalo's in that they did not have a strong community development organization such as PUSH in their neighborhoods before the start of Vacant to Vibrant. These neighborhoods had been in decline for several decades, and on the residential streets where we worked, the city was struggling to stay on top of housing abandonment and land vacancy. There was no prior experience with urban greening projects on these streets that residents could draw upon. As a result, it was more difficult to address resident expectations for an urban greening project. Residents were largely split between believing that the promised investment would not come, after countless broken promises in the years leading up to this project, or wanting one project to address all of the needs of their neighborhood. In contrast, in Buffalo, resident interest more closely scaled with project scope. Plans for Vacant to Vibrant were discussed at community meetings among a long docket of other topics for residents to weigh in on. Apart from the handball court, most concerns were hashed out between the community development organization and the project team and did not involve residents directly.

In Gary and Cleveland, in the absence of strong community development organizations that held regular public meetings, the project team interacted with residents directly. While residents in these cities had more opportunity for direct involvement with project decisions, fewer residents were engaged over the entire course of the project. A small number of residents were involved in the early planning stages, though at later stages they voiced concerns via their block organization and other community leaders. They were concerned about how the sites would look after installation, how they would be maintained, and whether the proposed new amenities might foster some of the worst activity of their neighborhoods. They were skeptical of the benefits of urban greening projects, even though benefits had been demonstrated in other cities. Residents believed in the exceptionalism of their cities—both good and bad—and doubted that lessons learned from other locations would transfer to Cleveland and Gary.

For urban greening practitioners in neighborhoods without prior experience with novel urban greening practices, it can be challenging to differentiate true dissatisfaction from the anxiety that normally accompanies change. In Vacant to Vibrant, we found that while the project team took the time to resolve some problems, other resident complaints worked themselves out as residents adjusted to a new normal. Noise complaints and general dissatisfaction with activity taking place on vacant lots that had been previously quiet often fell into this latter category. Complaints voiced by only one or two residents also tended to work themselves out over time. A small number of other complaints did not resolve spontaneously, however, and required action. Sometimes the only way to differentiate between real problems and anxiety about general change was to maintain open lines of communication and monitor complaints during an adjustment period, before devising a resolution.

Just as resident expectations for new investment can be high, the Vacant to Vibrant project team also had to maintain realistic expectations among team members about the amount of change that we could likely effect with a single initiative. Out of a desire to be helpful and create positive change, it was sometimes a challenge for the project team to not overcommit to solutions that we were unlikely to deliver on. Clearly defining our actual area of influence and sticking to problems that we could solve was better for building trust in the long run. With resident concerns that did overlap with our work, participating in neighborhood forums and community discussions, sharing information, and making connections were effective ways of being helpful within our area of influence without overcommitting. Based on these lessons, we would advise urban greening practitioners to weigh their involvement in deeper community issues carefully against how long they expect to be active in a community, and whether they have institutional support that will ensure the continuity needed to build and maintain trust for the long term.

Connectivity That Invites Unwanted Activity

Increased connectivity within and between neighborhoods, generally viewed as a positive attribute by city planners and landscape architects, was not viewed as desirable by residents in the Gary and Cleveland neighborhoods, who believed that connecting parcels to other streets would provide easy points of access for property damage and violent crime. Although connectivity has been shown to improve residents' health by making neighborhoods more walkable, studies show that residents are less likely to take advantage of walkable neighborhoods in areas with higher crime rates, out of fear. This fear is unlikely to be dissipated by three improved vacant lots within a neighborhood where the only other major investment is demolition. The benefits of urban greening projects do not start to manifest until neighborhoods reach a higher density of urban greening and other types of investment. In Cleveland, one study by the Center for Community Progress found that small urban greening projects had no significant effect on crime, housing values, or tax delinquency there, unlike projects in larger cities such as Philadelphia and New York. They attributed this to the low density of greening projects (1 percent of vacant lots) in a city with a weak housing market, where houses and vacant lots have relatively low market value.[6]

Examples from Vacant to Vibrant illustrate how resident concerns about crime led them to want less connectivity from urban greening, not more. In Gary, the back of the walled garden project abutted a large vacant lot—a wide, deep parcel that was still partly paved and overgrown. The main point of entry onto the lot was from Aetna Street, the main entrance to the neighborhood and a direct connection to the highway that ran to the north across the city. Over the course of the project's installation, a resident across the street became increasingly angry about how the recent demolition on the Vacant to Vibrant parcel had visually opened up his residential street to Aetna Street and beyond, which he feared would make his and neighboring houses more accessible for crime. Confirming his fears, an occupied house next door to the walled garden was broken into within the first year of project installation. While the project team initially looked at several options for closing the wall, this would have been only a superficial solution, due to easy access on adjacent parcels and several more planned demolitions of abandoned and dilapidated houses on the block. In the end, the city opted not to establish a precedent for fencing since they would not be able to offer it to future demolitions, and the wall was left open.

Similarly, in Cleveland, residents wanted to close the gap between two greened vacant parcels that presented a walkable connection between two parallel residential streets. In this neighborhood, older residents lived in fear of the youth from the public housing development to the north, as it had become more common in recent years for young men to hop back fences and chase each other (sometimes with handguns) through yards. The residents feared that growing connections between streets would make it easier for youth to travel south into the residential community, exposing more elderly residents to theft, burglary, and gang activity. As in Gary, this concern would only grow with increased house demolitions in the neighborhood, where ordinances required dilapidated fences along parcel boundaries to be removed along with the structures and driveways. In the end, this back parcel boundary was left open.

Whether as a means of separation of parks from yards next door, or to close gaps at the rear of parcels, fences were a frequent request before and after projects were completed. Given that fencing can represent a sizable portion of a small project budget and requires its own maintenance, the need for it should be carefully evaluated. Planning can consist of incorporating fencing into project budgets or, where that is not possible, initiating conversations with neighboring homeowners about their ability to purchase fencing for their own properties. Additionally, residents may be reassured by growing evidence that increased recreational use and appearance of care of urban green space increases real and perceived neighborhood safety over time.

Conflict and Disagreement within Neighborhoods

In Cleveland, Vacant to Vibrant projects uncovered tensions that existed in the neighborhood between homeowners, who tended to be seniors; renters, who tended to be younger and have children living with them; and residents of a large public housing development to the north. As discussed previously, these tensions first surfaced during project planning and continued through the life of the project. This was particularly in evidence at the pocket park, which abutted the back of the public housing development, separated by two unconnected seven-foot-tall chain-link fences. The back of the public housing development was bare lawn, and the space between the chain-link fences was a dumping site until it was cleaned up during installation of the stormwater park.

Removing mattresses and debris from the dumping site opened up sight lines to the swing set, and children aged five to twelve from the public housing development became adept at climbing both fences to reach the small park beyond. The residents of the neighborhood had been clear from the start that they did not want to attract residents of the public housing development to the park, but they had been more concerned about older youth. In truth, no one anticipated such an influx of young children. With no adults watching them, the kids seemed to be as entertained by destructive play as they were by using the site as intended. They scaled light poles and destroyed solar lighting; they peeled the illustration off site signage that explained stormwater management. But they were also swinging and playing and very frequently making use of the only play equipment they had access to, and they were genuinely having *fun* (figure 5-3). And, being such young children, they could create mischief but posed no real threat of harm.

Complaints about children from outside and within the neighborhood continued to be a point of disagreement among residents after installation. On a street with one lone pocket park, children's activity was concentrated in this one location. Noise, littering, and play spilled into neighbors' yards, disproportionately affecting a small number of residents. In an effort to be democratic in the planning stages of Vacant to Vibrant, we enlisted input from all residents on the street but had engaged residents adjacent to parcels more often than other residents.

Still, one area for future work is to determine how to appropriately weight feedback from residents adjacent to pocket parks, who will feel the impacts of community decisions more directly, against feedback from the broader community of residents who will make use of the space. In addressing resident disagreements, urban greening practitioners may need to navigate the line between helping to alleviate existing neighborhood problems and inadvertently fueling conflict between sectors of the community.

Figure 5-3. Children swing at the Vacant to Vibrant pocket park site in Cleveland.

Disconnect between Residents and Urban Greening Practitioners

Our nature play site in Cleveland highlights the messaging that residents attach to urban green space. While the play log, tire benches, and play mounds were intended to be whimsical play elements in an urban setting, the nature play design could not be visually separated from unkempt, abandoned, undervalued vacant land that surrounded it. Drawing lessons from private urban green space, the purpose of a residential yard is not only to provide a place for recreation but to add value to the home, communicate to onlookers that the land is owned and cared for, and communicate pride in the neighborhood. These messages do not always directly relate to the ecological value of yards, or of green space more generally.[7]

A challenge of ecologically friendly design is to strike a balance between communicating care and reducing the costs of maintenance. Sometimes experimental design projects target underutilized land because expectations for that land are lower, and residents or city government tolerate—or are unable to prevent—land uses that would not be allowed in wealthier neighborhoods. In our design process, we tried to stick to designs that had been used in a variety of contexts, including in more affluent neighborhoods. As with the example of the nature play lot, though, we sometimes failed to adequately consider how the context of the landscape we were working within could dramatically affect a project's reception. In talking with urban planners, landscape designers, and other urban greeners around the country about this lesson learned from Vacant to Vibrant, it seems likely that this context would not be commonly considered, because it is unfamiliar to many professionals who work in communities with high vacancy rates but live elsewhere.

When these neighborhoods were originally built by and for residents of specific ethnic groups, their ethnicities were reflected in the layout of the neighborhoods, the styles of the homes, and the types of businesses opened. Urban green space and other public spaces would have been constructed to serve the cultural needs and values of the community, and their appearance would have reflected residents' cultural heritage.

Today, there is little acknowledgment that urban neighborhoods continue to be heavily segregated along racial lines; in this failure to acknowledge racial segregation, there is also a false sense that urban greening projects are one-size-fits-all solutions for neighborhoods. Given that urban greening professionals are predominantly white and higher-income, as a first step we must acknowledge that we may not know how to design spaces to serve communities of color and/or lower-income communities.

Ultimately, such problems can be addressed by increasing the diversity of urban greening practitioners. In the meantime, we can include residents from the affected communities in the design process, and acknowledge areas where urban greening projects can be flexible to accommodate local preferences. This goes beyond being just a feel-good exercise—designing for existing communities helps ensure that the desired social outcomes of urban greening projects are achieved, and that their benefits are received by the residents who live near them. Given that many of the social benefits of urban greening are linked to reduced stress and increased physical activity, making projects welcoming is intrinsically linked to achieving project goals.

Lessons for Sustaining Urban Greening Projects

To be resilient to changes and threats across the life span of a project, urban greening initiatives are best aided by project teams and professional networks that are open, are collaborative, and have enough redundancy to withstand personnel changes. Such networks must be built on trust and goodwill, and this takes time. From our experience working within the Cleveland network of green stormwater infrastructure professionals, establishing shared goals or a vision for the collaboration can help individual members find their role and build group cohesion.

Maintenance requirements for urban green space can be challenging in any location, but in underserved neighborhoods within underfunded cities, where resources to support maintenance are slim, there is even more pressure to reduce these requirements. One way to do this is to simplify site plans; this requires greater transfer of knowledge from maintenance contractors to designers about the maintenance burden of landscape options, taking into consideration wear-and-tear, contractor maintenance capacity, and appearance. Communities that want to provide active play opportunities for young children should recognize the increased maintenance burden that such sites may create. Finally, although many green stormwater infrastructure plans default to using native plants, plant choices for green infrastructure should be intentional, taking into consideration both social and physical attributes of sites. Incorporating natives does not automatically reduce sites' maintenance requirements.

Three models for workforce development, demonstrated by Vacant to Vibrant project team members in Buffalo, Gary, and Cleveland, show how existing jobs can be adapted to become green jobs by providing experience and training in sustainable land use practices. There is recognized potential for green jobs to provide high-road employment opportunities—accessible to people with a variety of educational levels and life histories, with fair compensation and good benefits—to residents from underserved communities.

As urban greening professionals begin to generalize lessons from different initiatives to establish new urban greening best practices, we must be conscious of underlying assumptions about the physical and social attributes of sites that may affect the success of urban green space. In changing the landscape of neighborhoods, urban green space can provoke, coincide with, or unmask resident concerns that, at their base, relate to fears about the future of their communities. Principles of land use and connectivity from more affluent communities do not always directly translate to neighborhoods that have withstood long periods of disinvestment and decline. Urban greening professionals, as a group, may need to become more knowledgeable about the special needs of communities where vacant land is abundant and where residents do not have equitable access to urban green space. Such knowledge would help practitioners ensure that green space works toward neighborhood stabilization goals and serves the needs of the community that lives there.

6

Scaling Up Networks of
Small Green Infrastructure

The next stage of a pilot project such as Vacant to Vibrant is "scaling up" into something larger. For green stormwater infrastructure projects, an objective of scaling up is achieving measurable reductions in stormwater runoff, such as reducing total volume or peak flow, which is critical for sewer and stormwater systems. For urban greening projects, the purpose of scaling up is to achieve measurable effects on human health, property values, crime rates, and the environment. For vacant land reuse projects, scaling up means stabilizing home prices and slowing outward migration, foreclosure, abandonment, and demolition. For projects such as Vacant to Vibrant that sit at the intersection of stormwater management, urban greening, and vacant land use, any of these outcomes could be goals for scaling up.

For Vacant to Vibrant specifically, it is doubtful that scaling up will involve replicating the exact designs on vacant lots in large numbers. We have made design plans, software code, and other processes freely available so that projects can be replicated in other locations. To achieve the necessary scale, however, we would need a very large number of projects; replicating nine designs, or going through a community engagement process to identify custom designs, is not practical for hundreds or thousands of projects. Instead, we expect that the design elements and processes of Vacant to Vibrant will assist with the scaling up of urban greening practices more generally, by becoming threaded through a variety of urban greening approaches. We are already considering lessons about site selection for projects aiming to achieve goals such as increasing urban tree canopy or reducing mowing requirements for unimproved vacant lots.

In this book, we have selected lessons from Vacant to Vibrant that we believe to have the broadest applicability to a variety of urban greening projects. These lessons underlie larger needs, such as those listed here; that must be addressed to take urban greening to scale, which is the focus of this chapter.

- Evaluating the effectiveness of urban greening projects and making adjustments to design post-installation
- Connecting the dots between who pays for urban greening practices and who benefits, to reduce the effects of fragmentation of governing power[1] and responsibility[2]
- Enlisting the community, including installation and maintenance laborers, in shaping the design of projects to combat gentrification, strengthen neighborhoods, fit maintenance capacity, and meet expectations
- Promoting networks of small-scale urban greening projects and embedding green infrastructure in neighborhoods
- Elevating equitable urban green space to the level of long-term regional planning

Effectiveness of Green Infrastructure for Stormwater Management

In spite of early skepticism that green infrastructure could effectively manage stormwater runoff in urban areas, especially compared to gray infrastructure, green infrastructure has been shown to be an effective means of achieving stormwater control. For urban vacant lots, rain gardens may provide runoff control that exceeds what vacant land requires, except in locations where supplemental runoff can be routed into rain gardens from nearby impervious surfaces, such as roofs, parking lots, or roads (or where there are other obvious drainage issues). Instead, it may be less expensive, but sufficiently effective for stormwater management, to increase the permeability of existing soils by adding organic matter, such as leaf compost, to the top soil layer. Establishing good ground cover can further increase water loss via evapotranspiration and increase soil permeability by adding roots that channel water to deeper soil layers. With this in mind, the Vacant to Vibrant project team evaluated the performance of the rain gardens that were built into our nine project sites.

Measured Performance of Vacant to Vibrant Parcels

To evaluate the effectiveness of green stormwater infrastructure within Vacant to Vibrant project sites, we monitored the performance of rain gardens during June–November 2015 (figure 6-1).[3] A weather station was installed within each neighborhood to measure local climate conditions. Within the main rain garden at each parcel, and within nearby vacant parcels that were chosen because they shared site selection characteristics with project parcels, we monitored soil temperature just below the surface and soil moisture at three depths between 2 to 12 inches. This setup was an indirect means of evaluating runoff that reached the rain gardens, because directly measuring runoff under natural conditions is difficult without set points for water inflow and outflow. Pairing these measurements with estimates of rain garden capacity and runoff generated on each site, we could evaluate whether rain gardens ever filled with water based on whether soil probes recorded saturated soil conditions. (Unfortunately, monitoring wells that would have allowed us to directly observe water levels at deeper soil layers were lost to vandalism.)

Over the monitoring period, bioinfiltration soil mixes within rain gardens performed as intended—they infiltrated water very quickly—and rain gardens did not become filled with water. (Interestingly, while water infiltrated to deeper soil layers very quickly, we also observed a surprising amount of water being lost *upward* through the soil column between rain events; we will discuss this in more detail later.) Based on models of runoff that were generated on site and observations of precipitation and soil conditions within Vacant to Vibrant rain gardens, we estimated that project sites retained approximately 749,000 gallons of stormwater during the six-month observation period. Extrapolating from a Cleveland study

Figure 6-1. Vacant to Vibrant sites were outfitted with monitoring equipment to examine soil moisture fluctuations during natural storm events.

showing that it takes 7 to 11 gallons (or as few as 2 gallons, in select locations) of stormwater capture to mitigate 1 gallon of combined sewer overflow (CSO), reduction of CSO due to Vacant to Vibrant sites can be conservatively estimated at up to 180,000 gallons per year.[4]

Spread over nine sites among three cities, this is a modest level of stormwater capture relative to what the region requires. Our findings, however, support the concept of distributed stormwater management systems that have multiple other benefits to the community. In the Great Lakes region alone, where 24 billion gallons of CSO are generated per year, construction of 130,000 projects such as Vacant to Vibrant would be needed to alleviate regional CSO problems through green stormwater management practices alone.

While that number may be impractical (and accessing the quantity of land in strategic locations that would be required would require a radical shift in urban planning), it is a useful thought exercise to weigh the costs of such an undertaking—$2.4 billion at $18,000 each—against the costs of existing stormwater control programs to mitigate combined sewer overflow. The cost of the consent decree–related program to update the regional sewer system in northeast Ohio to mitigate 7.5 billion gallons of stormwater is estimated to be $3 billion over 25 years.[5] Considering that green infrastructure provides myriad social and environmental benefits to cities, a regional $2 billion investment in green stormwater infrastructure is more reasonable than it may seem at first glance.

CSO mitigation provides a useful example, but similar calculations of the financial costs and benefits of small networks of green infrastructure could be made for other parts of the US using the costs of drought, water transportation, flooding, crop failure, or other economic impacts of water surplus or scarcity. Rather than advocating for a pure green-infrastructure approach to water-related problems, though, these calculations make it clear that a hybrid approach—where green stormwater infrastructure can reduce the investment in gray system updates while also building neighborhood wealth in property values, human health, and climate change mitigation—is reasonable, if not essential.

Rethinking the Role of Plants in Stormwater Management
To justify greater flexibility about the types of plants used for green stormwater infrastructure, elsewhere in this book it has been mentioned that plants are assumed to have only a decorative role for stormwater best management practices and do not affect stormwater handling (figure 6-2). This assumption is based on (1) a lack of research about water loss due to evapotranspiration[6] for many types of plants outside of food crops, and

(2) the fact that the stormwater models used to specify the size of rain gardens and other stormwater control measures generally do not factor plants into their calculations. In these models, plants are assumed to have a constant effect, or are assumed to play too small a role for stormwater best management practices to consider them.

In monitoring water loss from soil in Vacant to Vibrant rain gardens over several months, at one rain garden in Buffalo that had a downspout disconnection and was planted in multi-stem dogwood, we observed up to 25 gallons of water being lost per day via evapotranspiration. So although stormwater capacity for rain gardens is assumed to be an engineering problem that only concerns the soil layer, in fact it is worthy of further study how plants that are chosen for rain gardens affect performance.

There is surprisingly little research on plant evapotranspiration rates outside of agricultural science. In the absence of such research, future work can test rain garden designs in which plants are assumed to have a functional role. Based on knowledge about how plants move water from the soil, practitioners can try to maximize water loss through evapotranspiration by choosing plants that grow quickly, have a lot of surface area, and have deep root systems. Trees are great for this purpose. In addition,

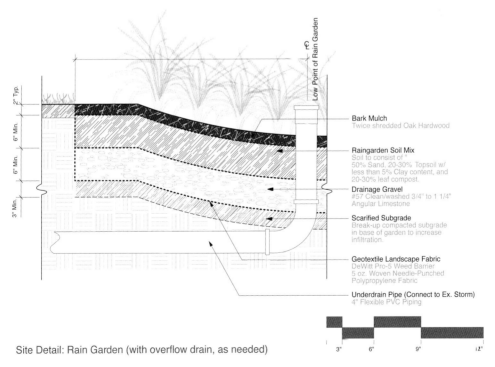

Site Detail: Rain Garden (with overflow drain, as needed)

Figure 6-2. Design plans for Vacant to Vibrant sites called for rain gardens containing two feet of stone and engineered soil to infiltrate surface water quickly.

practitioners may want to reconsider using plants that have built-in water retention features, such as waxy surfaces, that impede evapotranspiration. There are implications, too, for trying to minimize the amount of mulch that covers the soil surface, which impedes evaporation to keep moisture trapped within the soil. Using trees and woody shrubs, and decreasing the size of mulched areas, may have added benefits of reducing maintenance requirements.

Returning to findings from vacant land research that suggest that improving permeability of lots may be sufficient for stormwater control, there are more effective groundcovers for vacant parcels than traditional turf grass. Low-maintenance lawn mixes that contain yarrow, clover, and fine fescue or dwarf perennial rye grass perform well on vacant parcels in the Great Lakes and in northwest regions of the US. They green up quickly, are drought resistant, have deeper roots that improve water handling, and compete well with weeds. Traditional "no-mow" and other lawn mixes have been used on vacant parcels with some success, too, as long as instructions for planting are strictly followed. Such mixes have planting requirements that are similar to those of native plants grown from seed—fall or spring planting (fall is preferred), and normal maintenance (mowing and water) until establishment. Cutting corners during planting usually ends with poor results—so if conditions do not allow for strict adherence to planting instructions, it is often preferable to stick to traditional turf grass.

An additional practical suggestion for urban greening practitioners that is suggested from Vacant to Vibrant monitoring results is that, as engineered soils that promote infiltration become more commonly used in stormwater control measures, common rain garden plant recommendations may need to be adjusted in response. These engineered soil mixes do not hold water for long and can become very dry during periods of drought. Plants that do not tolerate dry soil conditions—which includes a lot of wetland and wet prairie plants that are often recommended for rain gardens—do not survive well in bioinfiltration mixes. In contrast, plants that tolerate well-drained soils and fluctuations in soil moisture are better adapted to these new soils. This may be counterintuitive to residents that have previously learned that rain gardens function as miniature wetlands—in fact, upland prairie plants may perform better in new infiltration soil mixes.

Location Effects on Green Infrastructure Performance
When developing methods for choosing project sites for Vacant to Vibrant, we factored in physical features that would facilitate cost-effective stormwater management. Soil type, topography, climate, and water table depth are natural attributes that can dramatically affect the cost-efficiency of stormwater management practices

by affecting how much stormwater runoff a site receives, making it difficult to draw direct comparisons about performance between two locations.

Even within the same geographic region, dramatic differences in soil types among the three Vacant to Vibrant neighborhoods highlighted differences in how stormwater management may need to be handled among the three cities. Working on vacant parcels in Gary, where soil is composed of 90 percent sand or more, raised questions about the purpose of stormwater management in areas where soil is highly permeable. Among sand dunes that parts of Gary were built upon, water infiltrates very quickly, leading to flooding from below as the water table rises. A high water table can add water to the combined sewer system through infiltration that may occur at breaks in the sewer line. Thus, in places such as Gary, during a rain or snowmelt event, stormwater management might mean holding water in the upper soil column to keep it from running off at the surface, and slowing it from reaching the water table. Addition of organic material, silt, and clay to the soil, as well as plants that absorb water quickly, can slow infiltration and improve loss of water through evapotranspiration.

Gary, Cleveland, and Buffalo are similar in their proximity to the Great Lakes and have similar climates. Differences among the cities in soil type and water table position, however, were not accounted for in planning for Vacant to Vibrant, highlighting an area for future work. In other areas of the US, where water is scarce during at least some parts of the year, the purposes of stormwater management may be to promote infiltration to recharge water tables, to retain water for use at other times of the year, or to slow runoff. These underlying, different needs for stormwater management must be considered during the exchange of lessons about effective practices between regions, because even simple best management practices, such as rain gardens, may serve very different purposes in different locations.

Connecting Costs and Benefits of Green Infrastructure

In a 2008 article that examined urban stormwater management in Australia and the US, a team of scientists identified common systemic barriers to sustainable urban stormwater management. Several of these barriers related to the costs of sustainable stormwater practices—uncertainties in cost, lack of funding and effective market incentives, and fragmentation of responsibilities among the different entities that are essential to implementing stormwater management.[6] These barriers may extend beyond stormwater management to urban greening projects more generally. Each of these barriers was a significant problem for the Vacant to Vibrant project in at least one city.

The benefits of urban green space have been listed in detail, and it is increasingly possible to attach a dollar amount to these benefits based on value added and costs avoided.[7] The value adds up quickly: In Cleveland, a conservative estimate of the value that an urban forest would provide to the community at 30 percent tree canopy is $44 million per year in improved air quality, energy savings, and health impacts, which in just a few years can exceed the cost of implementing a large-scale tree initiative to increase tree canopy from Cleveland's current value of 19 percent.[8] A more difficult problem for green infrastructure is that the people and entities who pay for it often do not reap enough of the financial benefits to cover their investment—the benefits are spread across the city. Because of the extent of public benefit, economists have recommended that green infrastructure projects be underwritten by public dollars.[9] In legacy cities with a shrinking tax base, however, there often is not enough public funding to build as much green infrastructure as is needed for even basic needs, such as regulatory compliance.

Contending with Fractured Responsibility

For Vacant to Vibrant and other urban greening projects, it is easier to connect the dots between investment and benefits in cities where there are close relationships between stakeholders who hold liability and stakeholders who receive benefits. When land banks, sewer authorities, and/or public health or public utilities are all contained within city government, as in Buffalo, the city land bank is able to complete housing demolition, which rolls into green stormwater infrastructure, which counts toward the city-owned sewer utility's consent decree. In this example, costs and benefits both go to the city. Similarly, the City of Gary owns vacant lots and pays for sewer updates that count toward their consent decree; they have also been able to make a persuasive case to funders that green stormwater infrastructure projects are part of a long-term economic development plan.

In Cleveland, in contrast, a nonprofit county land bank, which sits outside of local government, conducts house demolitions and passes vacant land to the city land bank. Separately, a regional sewer authority is liable for updates that count toward a regulatory mandate. Significant progress has been made toward better collaboration between these three entities, but there have been difficulties among them when, for example, the city is liable beyond their ability to pay for maintenance of trees and rain gardens that have been installed by the county land bank, or when disputes arise between the city and the regional sewer authority over who is responsible for paying for road repaving when sewer work is timed to coincide with scheduled road maintenance.

In cities with shrinking tax bases, where liability is fractured among several entities, it can be difficult to coordinate green infrastructure projects at a scale large
enough to create significant change. In these cities, accounting must be sufficiently
detailed to capture costs and benefits for all parties involved to make the case for
cooperation. Consent decrees have been used successfully by the US Environmental
Protection Agency to make cities better account for the costs of gray infrastructure
maintenance and updates. The cost of updating sewer systems to meet compliance
standards has encouraged many sewer authorities to implement stormwater fees,
which is one way to share the financial burden of water treatment among civic actors
whose land use decisions impact the amount of water that must be treated. Going a
step further, stormwater credits that allow ratepayers to get a reduced bill, by mitigating runoff from their property that reaches the sewer system, can create financial
incentives for best management practices. As stormwater fees are relatively new in
the US, they are usually only a fraction of the amount needed to make stormwater
management a financially sound investment for all but the largest landowners.

At the level of big-box stores with large surface parking lots, regional religious institutions, or school districts, stormwater fees have created more incentive for green infrastructure. In Cleveland, stormwater fees have encouraged city departments to invest
in more green stormwater infrastructure to offset large bills from public housing and
municipal buildings. (In contrast, it would take an average residence several years to
recoup the costs of implementing stormwater management from credits alone.)

Taken even further, stormwater credits that are tradable among ratepayers can
create a system that incentivizes stormwater best management practices where they
are most needed, by installing green infrastructure in high-need areas and selling
those credits to other ratepayers who cannot, or choose not to, install them on their
own property.[10] Tradable credits are mostly still in the pilot phase in the places where
they exist, and there remain questions about how to calculate the cap on stormwater
credits across an entire sewershed (where a cap is one necessary half of a "cap-and-
trade" system). As energy costs and water management needs are certain to rise in
many areas in the US as a result of climate change, stormwater fees are likely to rise
with them, creating more financial incentive for innovative credit systems.

Expanding the List of Stakeholders

Better accounting of urban greening benefits creates ways to engage stakeholders in
helping offset the burden of project costs. Increasingly, hospitals, insurance companies, and public health agencies are understanding the value of urban greening practices for improving health outcomes for clients. Urban tree canopy has been shown

to be positively linked to respiratory and cardiac health; fewer hospital admissions and deaths occur in areas with greater tree canopy. The recent spread of emerald ash borer, which has resulted in 10 percent loss of tree canopy among many cities and higher localized rates of tree loss in neighborhoods that were heavily planted in ash trees, has provided evidence of a causal relationship: 6,000 deaths due to respiratory illness and 15,000 deaths due to cardiac disease between 1990 and 2007 have been attributed to loss of urban tree canopy due to emerald ash borer in midwestern and eastern states.[11] Utilities companies also have begun investing in trees in urban areas to reduce energy loads from heating and cooling. The Arbor Day Foundation has helped make it easier for utilities to pay directly for trees by connecting them to private landowners via a turnkey web tool.[12]

Urban greening costs can also be split according to functional parts, with separate accounting (and funding sources) divided among separate stakeholder groups. Consider a rain garden: The stormwater management function is dictated by the grade and characteristics of the soil; stormwater management agencies can pay for these components. The addition of decorative plants, or trees that provide other ecological benefits enhances the rain garden but is not necessary for its function; these costs could be shared by community development or ecology-minded groups. Trees could be purchased by health-related funding sources. Recreation equipment, such as benches or play equipment, could be paid for separately by the stakeholders who want them. People United for Sustainable Housing (PUSH) Buffalo has successfully shown that installation and maintenance costs can be rolled into a green workforce development program and social enterprise business.

Although it requires more work to pull these separate funding sources together, for multipurpose urban greening projects such as Vacant to Vibrant, this approach better connects costs and benefits and may provide a source of financial stability in the long run. In cities with limited funding to support infrastructure improvements, cost-sharing may make scaling up more feasible.

Overcoming Opportunity Cost

In urban areas where different parties are competing for land, one argument against scaling up urban greening projects concerns opportunity cost.[13] Even in cities with weak housing markets, where there is little near-term interest in developing large numbers of vacant lots, urban greening on vacant land is often viewed as an interim strategy until development pressure grows again, rather than as a permanent strategy for building healthy neighborhoods. The cost of losing a housing development or other tax-generating use for vacant lots keeps city planners from committing to urban greening as a permanent land use.

Opportunity cost is highest in neighborhoods where housing markets are relatively strong. Community gardens and pocket parks are being removed from these areas to make room for development. In densely developed neighborhoods, stormwater control measures often occur as retrofits on streets or on existing development, where access to these features is less than to public parcels developed as urban green space, reducing the public benefit of such investment.

To make the case for urban green space in all communities, opportunity cost must be directly compared with the social and economic benefits provided by urban green space, future market demand for walkable neighborhoods, and the amount of undeveloped land that must remain for climate mitigation. Vacant to Vibrant demonstrates the feasibility of layering multiple land uses into small lots, which may make a stronger case for offsetting opportunity cost by combining recreation and stormwater management to increase the public benefit that small lots provide. In places that are reluctant to turn away developers, multifunctional green space may be a key to offsetting opportunity cost.

Reducing Green Infrastructure Costs

As green stormwater infrastructure becomes more commonly used, there is room to reduce its per-unit cost. At present, green stormwater infrastructure installation costs vary widely because factors that affect cost—performance standards, methods, funding sources—are themselves highly variable. For Vacant to Vibrant, we wanted to keep installation costs low in the interest of replicability in locations with limited funding. Our projects varied in cost from $7,000 to $35,000 per parcel, with an average cost of about $18,000 each. Maintenance costs are $1,000 to $2,000 per lot per year. (These costs exclude the unforeseen major modifications that were made after installation, such as on the nature play lot in Cleveland.) While some green stormwater control measures of a similar size have cost $80,000 or more, when compared to the clean-and-green approach to neighborhood beautification that has been used in cities such as Philadelphia, Vacant to Vibrant costs are still higher than most city governments or community organizations could afford to implement on a very large scale.

As more stormwater management authorities are funding green stormwater infrastructure, reasonable costs are being evaluated in terms of performance and are being weighed against gray infrastructure alternatives. Although green infrastructure is frequently touted as a low-cost alternative to gray infrastructure, in actual practice the costs of green infrastructure relative to its performance—commonly measured in cost per gallon of stormwater treated, or cost per gallon of CSO mitigated—vary widely. The installation costs of Vacant to Vibrant projects ranged from $0.06 to $0.19 per gallon of stormwater captured, which translates to an estimated $0.58 to $1.95 per gallon of CSO mitigated (see table 4-1). Target costs for stormwater capture vary by location, based on energy costs associated with water treatment, the type of stormwater management that is needed, and the amount of precipitation. In Cleveland, an average of $1.51 per gallon was considered an acceptable target for stormwater capture that included green infrastructure, compared to $0.75 per gallon for gray infrastructure–only methods.[14]

The location of Vacant to Vibrant projects greatly affected the amount of stormwater captured, and the cost-per-gallon of stormwater treated, due to spatial fluctuations in runoff that could be routed to rain gardens. Location influenced cost efficiency at three spatial scales. At the level of the area immediately surrounding the rain garden—its catchment area—the opportunity to add downspout disconnections or curb cuts greatly affected cost-per-gallon measures, because these are inexpensive methods to divert a relatively large amount of surface runoff. For example, addition of a downspout or curb cut to Vacant to Vibrant projects could route relatively large amounts of additional stormwater to rain gardens at an added capital cost of around $0.25 per gallon.

In Cleveland, city government was nervous about liability for downspout disconnections related to the transfer of stormwater across parcel boundaries and, especially, from resident-owned parcels onto city-owned parcels. In the end, the city decided it did not want the liability and long-term maintenance concerns related to diverting runoff onto their property. Cleveland city government was also concerned about responsibility for long-term maintenance—the local sewer authority had examples of establishing curb cuts, but only on parcels they owned and for which they had assumed permanent responsibility.

Similarly, Gary city government rejected proposals to incorporate downspout disconnections due to maintenance and liability concerns about the downspouts themselves: Who would maintain gutters and pipes, and who would be responsible if they clogged with leaves and debris.

Vacant to Vibrant was able to incorporate downspout disconnections at some sites in Buffalo, where the community development organization owned both the rental house and the vacant lot adjacent to it. From these experiences, it would seem that downspout disconnections to vacant lots are easiest to do when ownership is consistent between the two parcels.

Finding solutions to these concerns would have greatly improved the cost-effectiveness of our green stormwater infrastructure. Possible workarounds for future projects include deliberately selecting project sites where stormwater is transferred between parcels that have the same ownership—for example, incorporating stormwater management features into resident side yards, or diverting runoff from municipally owned buildings onto adjacent municipally owned vacant lots. Additionally, concerns about future development could be addressed by creating policies that detail how rain gardens and curb cuts should be handled in the event of lot transfer and future development.

At larger spatial scales, at the level of the sewershed, the cost per gallon of water treated by green infrastructure is influenced by sewershed boundaries that dictate the interceptor, water treatment facility, or CSO to which runoff ultimately flows. In Cleveland, where large storage tunnels within select sewersheds will eventually direct all stormwater runoff to water treatment facilities instead of CSOs, green infrastructure is rendered unnecessary from a CSO mitigation perspective but may still be useful for reducing water treatment costs. An important consideration is that sewersheds vary in their sensitivity to stormwater runoff. In some Cleveland sewersheds, for example, it takes only 7 gallons of stormwater runoff to produce 1 gallon of CSO.[15] In other sewersheds with different terrain and sewer structures, it takes 12 gallons of runoff to create 1 gallon of CSO. (At localized areas within these watersheds, however, the ratio can be as low as 2:1.) Green infrastructure thus has larger effects on CSO production in sewersheds where less water is needed to trigger overflows, driving per-gallon costs of CSO mitigation down.

We considered some of these factors in the placement of Vacant to Vibrant projects, but with lessons learned and new data available, factoring in site ownership and terrain can greatly improve the cost efficiency of green stormwater infrastructure. Ultimately, such considerations will be needed to scale green infrastructure up to a level where it is a viable alternative to large gray-infrastructure investments if cost-per-gallon measures continue to be a compelling factor that drives decision making.

Community Engagement

In the long term, scaling up green infrastructure will require continued community engagement to infuse more considerations for ecological health into resident preferences for urban landscapes, while also ensuring that urban greening practices work in service of existing communities by reflecting their values and culture.

Low Maintenance Is Not Low Value

As discussed earlier, one challenge of promoting low-maintenance, ecologically friendly landscapes in urban areas is that such landscapes are perceived to have inherently low social value. This is for two reasons. First, maintenance requirements can be an indication of wealth and status, so higher-maintenance landscapes are often perceived to be more desirable.[16] Consider a golf course or a royal garden: we perceive these landscapes to be aesthetically pleasing in part because of the labor required to cultivate their uncommonness—strange plants in strange shapes in incongruent places. Exotic species, topiaries, and lush gardens in deserts all require special skills and intense labor to survive; the ability to sustain them usually requires wealth and prestige. On a more modest scale, a turf lawn—green and weed-free—communicates that the homeowner has the time and resources to cultivate a space that is very different from what would grow spontaneously.

Secondly, people do not reliably factor ecological health into their perception of landscape value.[17] Americans are, in general, very poorly educated about plants, which leads to the inability to notice them in our landscape, a phenomenon known as "plant blindness." People who have not had formal training in plants tend not to notice indicators of lower ecological integrity, such as invasive species, low biodiversity, or signs of past human disturbance. Urban dwellers may even prefer ecologically unfriendly practices, leading them to limit plant biodiversity through weeding or use of herbicides. Monoculture lawns exemplify this practice. Look, too, at the limited palette of common landscaping plants compared to the wide range of options available. Even ornamental grasses are relative newcomers to urban yards, where preference has been given to hostas, shrubs, and trees.

More ecologically minded folks can forget how common plant blindness is. In a land of golf courses and turf lawns, patches of native prairie may seem alien. The negative perceptions of intentionally low-maintenance landscapes—that they are weedy, ugly, and an indicator of disinvestment—are not inconsequential. While tidier urban greening practices have been shown to lower stress (which can improve human health and violent crime statistics) and raise property values, unkempt vacant lots have the opposite effect.[18] The negative social and economic effects of such lots on neighborhoods directly result from the value that urban residents attach to maintenance requirements and appearance.

In declining neighborhoods that have long suffered the consequences of disinvestment, there are ethical considerations for creating landscapes that convey a lack of care (whether intentionally or not). In general, if a landscape practice would not be tolerated by residents of more stable, wealthier neighborhoods, where it would be less likely to cause measurable negative effects on property values, it is arguably unethical to construct them in areas that are more vulnerable to these negative impacts.

This is not to suggest, however, that low-maintenance urban greening practices should not be used in declining neighborhoods, where they are most needed—in fact, we located Vacant to Vibrant within neighborhoods that could benefit from the stabilization effects of urban greening practices. Instead, in the interest of using low-maintenance urban greening practices in an ethical manner, we should build them in a way that is sensitive to localized cultural norms. Over time, such projects can shift the needle on how low-maintenance requirements are perceived and close the gap between ecological value and aesthetic value.

Shifting Public Opinion about Low-Maintenance Urban Landscapes

Academic literature suggests three ways to bring aesthetic value and ecological function of landscapes into closer alignment: educational campaigns, good design practices, and making use of early adopters to shift public perception.[19] Of these, urban greening practitioners often focus energies on education, with the belief that if they simply tell residents the story of how rain gardens clean water and provide habitat, residents who find rain gardens unattractive will abandon that attitude. While education can increase residents' preference for ecologically friendly landscapes,[20] it is just one component of a multipronged approach to shifting cultural norms on landscapes to include more eco-friendly practices.

Good design can convey care and intentionality, such as through the use of tidy borders, which increase tolerance for the untidy spaces within them. A tidy border can be a mown strip, possibly with the addition of a simple fence (as in the Philadelphia LandCare program). In Vacant to Vibrant, we experimented with several types of low-cost decorative fencing, including cable fences, zigzag chain-link fences, and bollard fences. To reduce fence upkeep and grow urban tree canopy, in Cleveland and Detroit there are trials of living bollard fences composed of trees planted in a row. Aside from borders, an approach that our community partner PUSH found to create a tidy appearance while also easing maintenance requirements in Buffalo involved two techniques: limiting the number of plant species used and keeping plants spaced apart in a bed of composted wood mulch. They used native plants that could be perceived as weedy in other contexts, but in a manner which still conveyed that the space was being maintained.

Lastly, there is evidence that the biggest influence on residents' behavior is the actions of their neighbors. Neighbors have been found to be highly influential in shaping a wide range of behavior, such as lowering household energy consumption,[21] displaying political yard signs,[22] and tolerating eco-friendly landscapes.[23] Early adopters of sustainable land use practices can serve as ambassadors to shift public opinion over time. For practitioners, cultivating relationships with willing neighbors may be as important as trying to sway public opinion through educational campaigns.

Communicating Culture

Urban greening projects can help communities protect and convey their cultural heritage as cities begin to redevelop, without contributing to gentrification, if they are designed to serve the residents who currently live there.[24] Although it is fashionable to use decorative bunchgrasses and prairie forbs in rain gardens, stormwater management features have the flexibility to feature plants that reflect the local community. In Vacant to Vibrant neighborhoods, the fashionable types of plants were not well liked and, at two sites, were removed by residents. A community-based landscape contractor is a good resource for guidance on plants that are popular, will meet project objectives, and will withstand local threats, be they soil conditions, herbivores, theft, or rough play. In areas where traditional lawn aesthetics are firmly entrenched, stormwater control measures can be planted with manicured lawns and ornamental trees, if community resistance means that is the only way to implement green stormwater infrastructure.

In neighborhoods that are receiving new investment, residents can be sensitive to the cumulative effects of outside influences—funders, organizations, government, contractors—on their community culture. In communities of color that have historically been excluded from economic prosperity, urban greening projects can reignite old fears of exclusion. While residents are happy for investment, they also worry that such projects signal changes that will eventually push them out. These fears may be particularly strong when project leaders are white and/or unfamiliar with the community.

In the city of Gary, in recognition of historical inequities and to ensure that economic prosperity works for its residents, projects are required to enlist local contractors and materials as much as possible. For Vacant to Vibrant, the installation contractor from a neighboring city worked with the city's Urban Conservation Team to help prepare and finish sites. The contractor also hosted the Urban Conservation Team on site to observe technical parts of installation, such as the construction of rain gardens.

Workforce development programs are another way for urban greening projects to support the community. While it can be difficult to find reliable funding to support project maintenance, more funding opportunities are available to support green workforce development. These programs can take on project maintenance while building a pipeline for community members to access high-road green jobs.

Building Large Urban Networks of Small Green Infrastructure

Embedding green infrastructure into urban neighborhoods will require systems-level change in what green space is allowed to look like, what it is allowed to do, how much of it there is, where it is located, and who supports it. There are tangible barriers to this kind of systemic change, including funding bottlenecks and outdated city ordinances that do not allow for new green technology, as well as conceptual barriers to change, such as assumptions that future urban development patterns should resemble those of the past. Pushing cities in the direction of smart (re)development will require an entrepreneurial spirit—implementing urban greening practices in an iterative way, quickly incorporating lessons learned, and adapting messaging to take advantage of changing funding priorities while remaining anchored to basic principles, such as sustainability, equity, and practicality. Practitioners could also benefit from the development of new tools that streamline decision making, and from expanding professional networks to learn from—and advocate with—a broader array of collaborators.

Updating Policy to Allow for New Practices
In many cities, ordinances are still in place that prohibit or severely restrict a variety of sustainable land use practices. For example, cities may prohibit downspout disconnections from the sewer or stormwater system, placing an unnecessary burden on gray infrastructure while restricting the effectiveness of green infrastructure. Or cities may require overflow drains that connect to the sewer system on even the smallest of green infrastructure installations. Ordinances such as these are gradually being updated or removed as more cities demonstrate good outcomes. For example, within the course of the Vacant to Vibrant project, in Buffalo we observed city requirements for green infrastructure moving from requiring overflows to the sewer system for all projects, to requiring them only in certain instances, to eliminating them for almost all projects, even those located close to the right-of-way. As a next step to removing restrictions, new policies can be put in place to incentivize or require green practices such as protecting or planting trees or ensuring a minimum level of stormwater capture.

The growing body of research that demonstrates the effectiveness of green infrastructure has helped advance policy, but it is often less compelling to policymakers than direct experience gained through site visits and pilot projects. As such, there can be a lot of pressure placed on practitioners in cities where urban greening practices are new to create successful pilot projects, even if those practitioners may be inexperienced in implementing practices themselves and existing policies contain ample barriers to project success. Growing regional and national professional networks are helping spread sustainable practices to new cities by connecting less experienced professionals to counterparts in other locations who can share direct experience; such networks exist for urban forestry, urban farming, and green stormwater infrastructure.

For practitioners who are new to sustainable practices, whether they are designers, landscape contractors, project managers, or community organizers, there is benefit in tapping into topical professional networks to lower the chances that an unfavorable project outcome sets local government back several years in its willingness to entertain new sustainable practices. Practitioners should allocate project manager time to closely monitor subcontractors too, to ensure that they adhere to instructions and thus avoid costly failures and setbacks to adoption. Project managers who can be present on site to guide implementation are preferable for this reason.

Embedding Urban Greening into Neighborhood Fabric

In post-industrial cities that are expected to weather the current economic downturn and someday regain population, there is often an unspoken assumption that many vacant residential lots will one day be redeveloped back into the same types of housing they used to support. Building out neighborhoods of standalone single-family homes risks both repeating past mistakes and ignoring future threats from climate change. A more ecologically sound approach for climate resilience is to increase housing density while expanding the amount of green space contained within neighborhoods. This type of neighborhood development has lower energy consumption compared to low-density housing such as single-family homes; encourages recreation, walking, and bicycling; and provides cleaner air and water.

In post-industrial cities that are afraid of discouraging developers and potential homebuyers, there is a perception that higher-density housing has less market appeal. The US is already in the midst of a cultural shift in how we envision urban living, however. In the past three surveys conducted by the National Association of Realtors, a majority of respondents from large metro areas stated a preference for smaller, attached homes in walkable neighborhoods.[25] Younger adults are looking for shorter and alternative ways of getting to work, while older generations are shifting toward neighborhoods and living formats with higher walkability as they age and downsize from multilevel single-family homes. These market demands present an opportunity for post-industrial cities to build new housing that satisfies modern desires and includes ample urban green space, rather than re-creating past neighborhood formats.

Elevating Permanent Green Space Preservation to Long-Term Regional Planning

On the flip side of manufacturing loss is an opportunity for post-industrial US cities to reinvent themselves as vibrant urban areas, where clean green space serves the economy, residents, and the environment. At a time when Rust Belt cities are planning for redevelopment, there is a window of opportunity to build healthier neighborhoods that have adequate green space for recreation, stormwater control, cleaner air, milder temperatures, and better human health outcomes. Historically, private and public green space has typically been lost as cities grow and development density increases, due to planning methods that do not adequately account for green space conservation and planning.[26] Large, dense US cities, such as Philadelphia, New York, and Chicago, are retrofitting green space to handle stormwater management, urban heat island mitigation, and urban forests. Planning now to preserve land from development—including designation of how much land needs to be preserved, and where—will ensure that post-industrial cities have adequate green space for future needs.

Just as fragmentation of responsibility among many different organizations makes it difficult to take urban greening projects to scale (see chapter 5), fragmentation of urban greening sectors impedes the ability of practitioners to elevate discussions about urban green space to the level of city and regional planning. If urban farmers, urban foresters, native species advocates, and stormwater managers are unable to gain traction in planning discussions separately, perhaps working in collaboration would catalyze a more effective campaign for large-scale, long-term green space preservation.

There are added benefits of working more closely. Urban greening sectors can learn from one another—for example, urban farmers can share social justice lessons with stormwater managers, and urban forestry decision-making tools can be adapted to other types of green infrastructure. Parks is one green sector that is already heavily engaged with regional planning efforts; other groups can leverage interests that are shared with parks advocates to benefit from the position that parks have obtained at regional planning tables. The Vacant to Vibrant initiative demonstrates potential overlap between recreation and stormwater management; parks also have natural synergies with urban forestry and native species preservation. Likewise, urban agriculture and community gardens have successfully lobbied for space allocation within dense urban areas such as New York City and Los Angeles. There is potential to learn from, and build alliances with, urban agriculture—which often has strong community organizing roots—for mutual benefit of residents and green stormwater infrastructure, urban tree canopy, and native plants.

In cities with abundant vacant land, spatial data analysis can guide decision making about preserving vacant lots as urban green space. Urban forestry provides a good example of the power of spatial tools for instigating change. Dozens of cities throughout the US have created large-scale plans for tree planting and maintenance to grow their urban tree canopy, thanks to a suite of free and paid toolkits, software, and guidance documentation aimed at decision makers. Such products help cities understand the value of their urban canopy and help them set and achieve goals for increased canopy. Examples of tools include the i-Tree software suite from the USDA Forest Service, as well as canopy assessments and goal-setting resources from American Forests. The tangible value of urban tree canopy that these tools help demonstrate has led to innovations in funding mechanisms for tree planting and maintenance, such as recommendations that tree initiatives become part of urban health budgets. More recently, tools to allow cities to take stock of their parks have spurred the creation of initiatives to place quality parks within a 10-minute walk of every resident,[27] and cities such as Philadelphia are using spatial analysis to plan networks of green stormwater infrastructure.[28] In New York state, spatial analysis of suitability of vacant land for different land uses is now being factored into statewide, long-term green space planning.[29]

If these tools could be combined and expanded upon, they could constitute a comprehensive, data-driven decision-making aid for urban green space that could guide regional long-term planning around the number and location of vacant parcels that should be earmarked for permanent preservation. Just as cities have been able to plan for expansion of the urban tree canopy by identifying areas that need air quality improvement, and translating that into the number of trees required, a suite of software could guide decisions about the quantity and placement of stormwater capture, carbon storage, air quality improvement, and temperature regulation that will be needed to address future social and environmental change. Such calculations of existing and potential social and environmental benefits are needed to provide compelling arguments against development. At the level of regional planning, these data can guide decisions about the quantity and distribution of vacant land that will be needed to meet the urban priorities of walkable, healthy neighborhoods, equity, and climate resilience.

The Vacant to Vibrant initiative demonstrates the value and feasibility of repurposing urban vacant land as green space that balances social and ecological priorities for neighborhoods. Scaling up projects such as Vacant to Vibrant into large networks of small-scale urban green space will require closer attention to performance and cost efficiency to compete with gray infrastructure investment; layering of green land uses to increase the value of benefits they provide, to preserve land in the face of development pressure; spatial tools that can match the benefits of urban green space to neighborhood need and land potential; and more intentional coordination among urban greening professionals with expertise in different sustainable land use practices.

The opportunity contained within growing and more equitably distributing urban green space is the ability to change the structure of cities to better serve people and the environment. In post-industrial cities, multipurpose urban green space on vacant land can be one approach to help alleviate neighborhood decline and mitigate the costs of updating aging infrastructure. Urban green space that is designed in collaboration with residents, to serve their needs and reflect their culture, is a chance to strengthen communities that have been historically excluded from economic prosperity. In cities throughout the US, urban greening projects such as Vacant to Vibrant can be incorporated into strategies to support healthy, walkable neighborhoods that are resilient to economic, community, and environmental changes across the urban life cycle.

Appendix

This appendix includes site layout plans, stormwater management plans, and planting plans for each of the Vacant to Vibrant project installation sites.

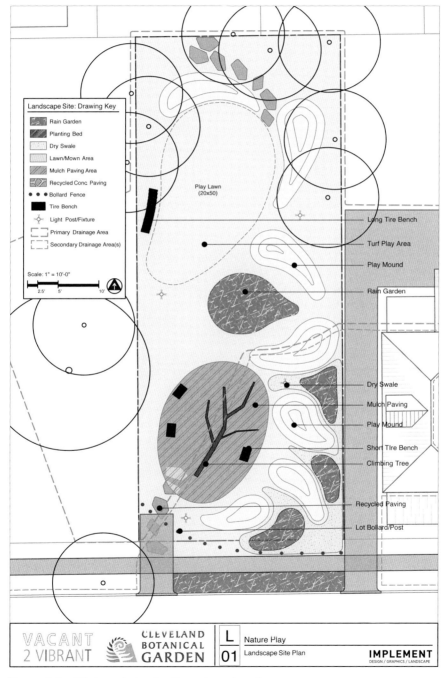

Figure A-1a. Site layout plan for the nature play site.

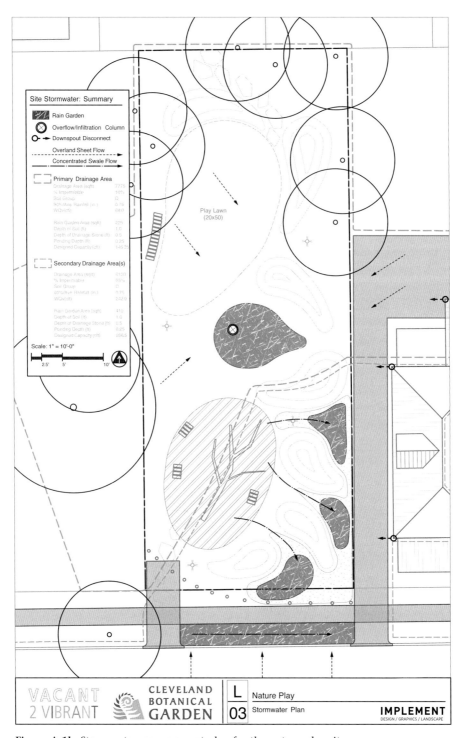

Figure A-1b. Stormwater management plan for the nature play site.

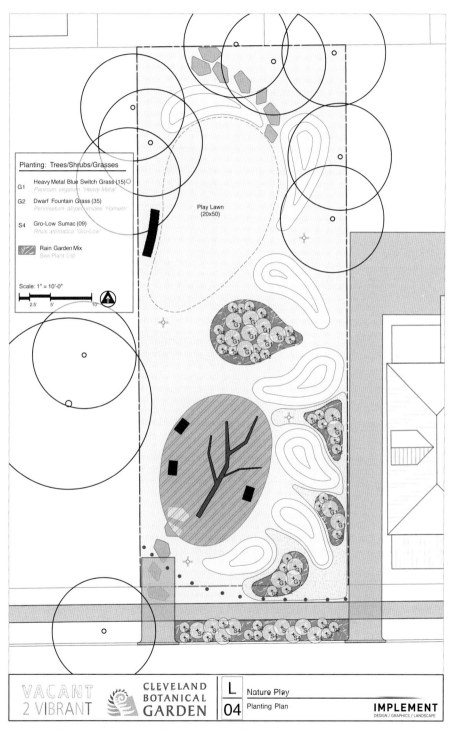

Figure A-1c. Planting plan for the nature play site.

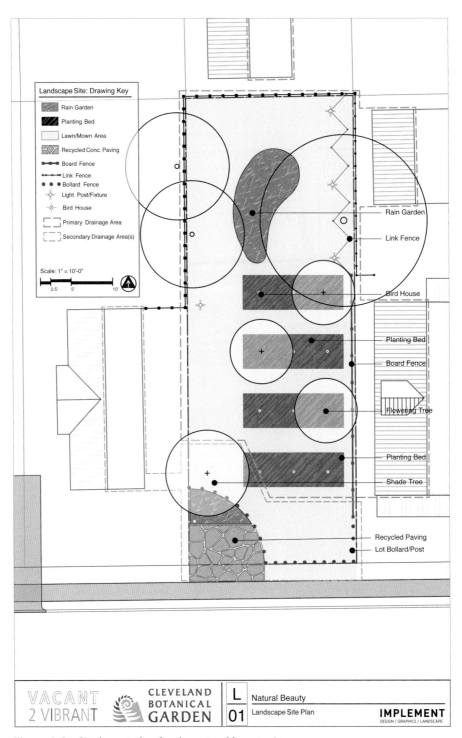

Figure A-2a. Site layout plan for the natural beauty site.

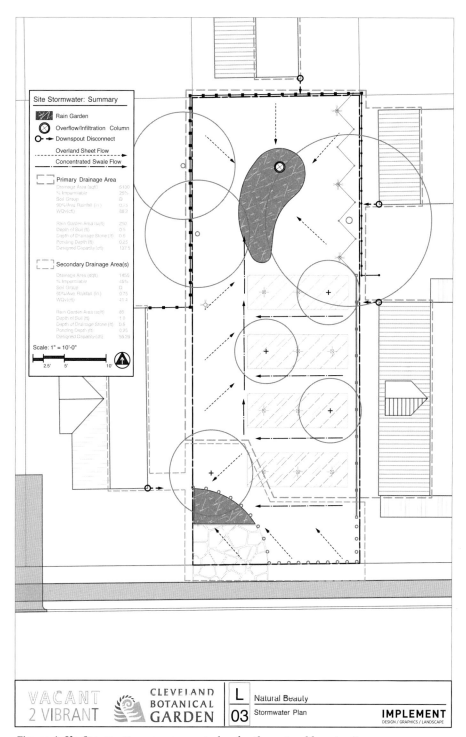

Figure A-2b. Stormwater management plan for the natural beauty site.

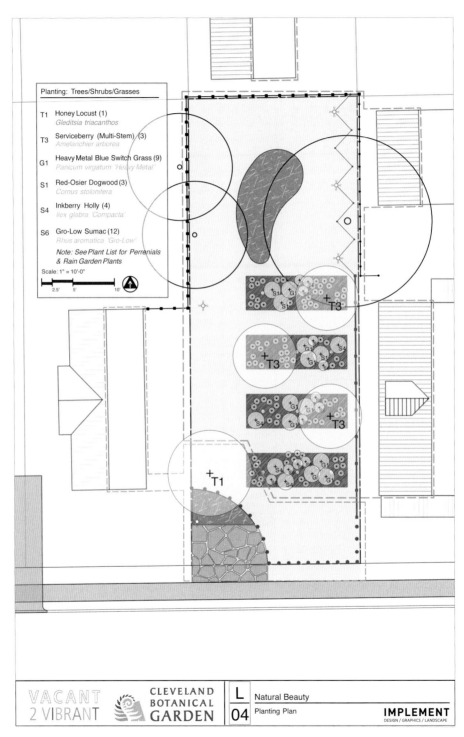

Figure A-2c. Planting plan for the natural beauty site.

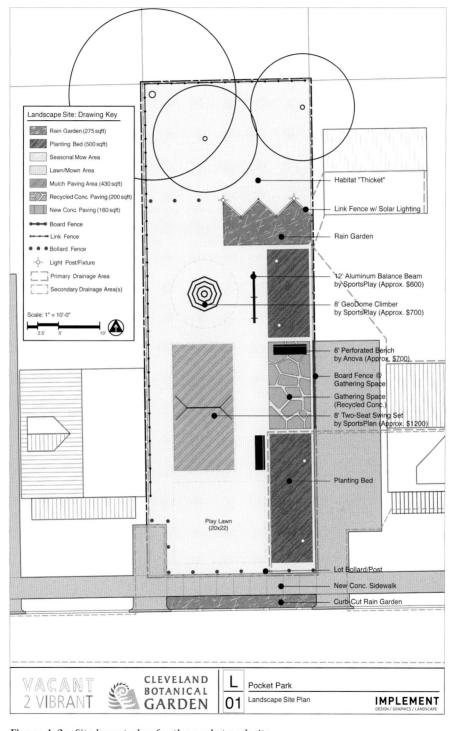

Figure A-3a. Site layout plan for the pocket park site.

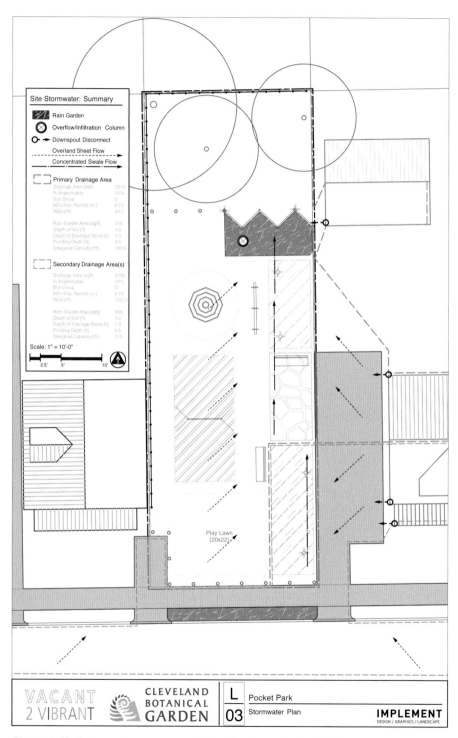

Figure A-3b. Stormwater management plan for the pocket park site.

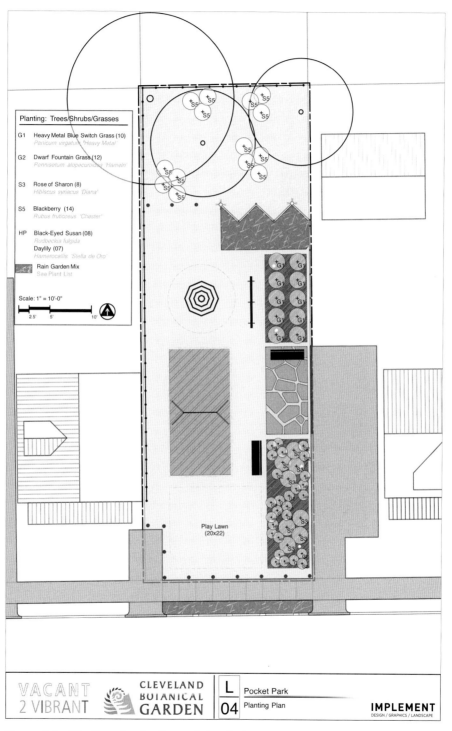

Figure A-3c. Planting plan for the pocket park site.

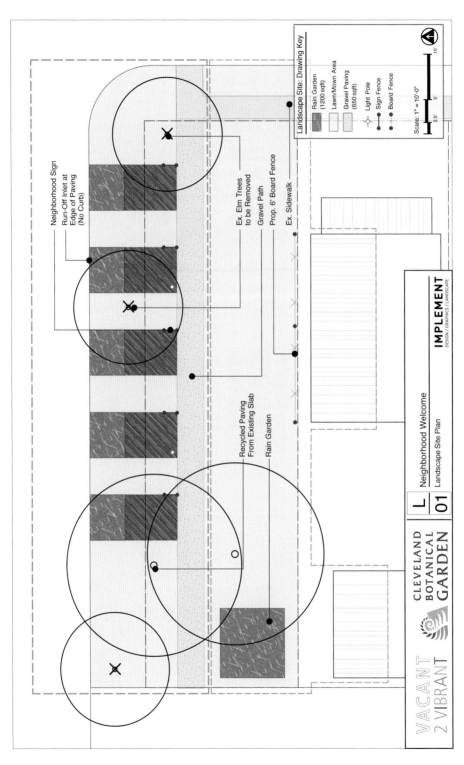

Figure A-4a. Site layout plan for the neighborhood welcome site.

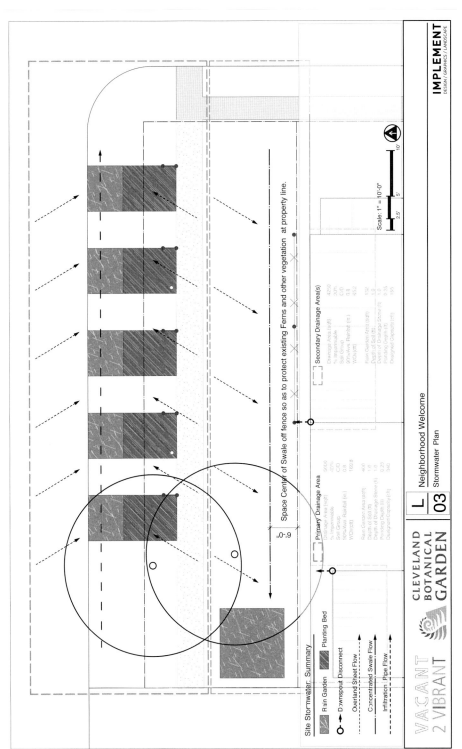

Figure A-4b. Stormwater management plan for the neighborhood welcome site.

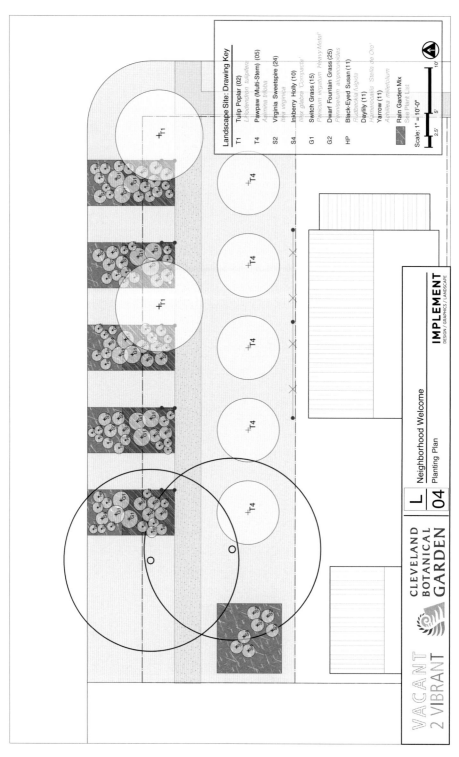

Figure A-4c. Planting plan for the neighborhood welcome site.

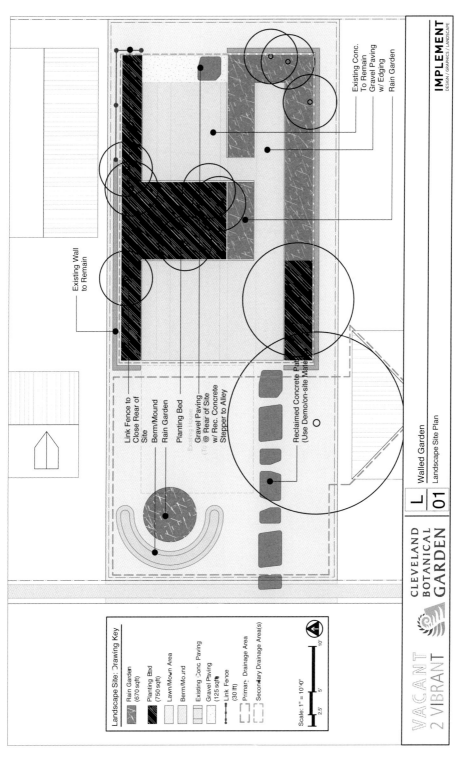

Figure A-5a. Site layout plan for the walled garden site.

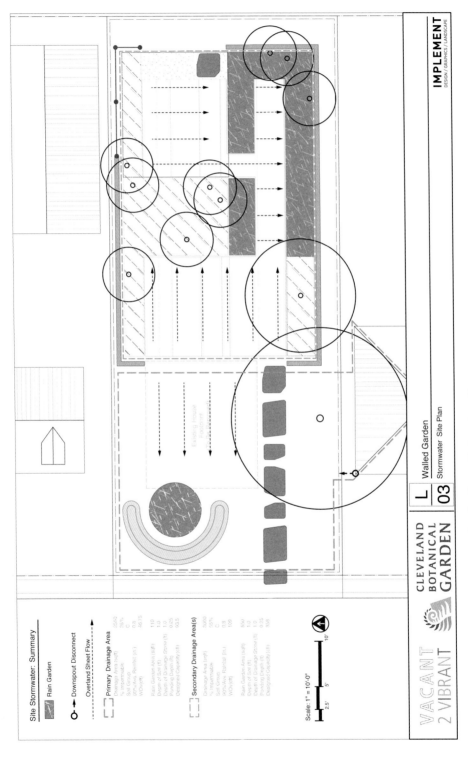

Figure A-5b. Stormwater management plan for the walled garden site.

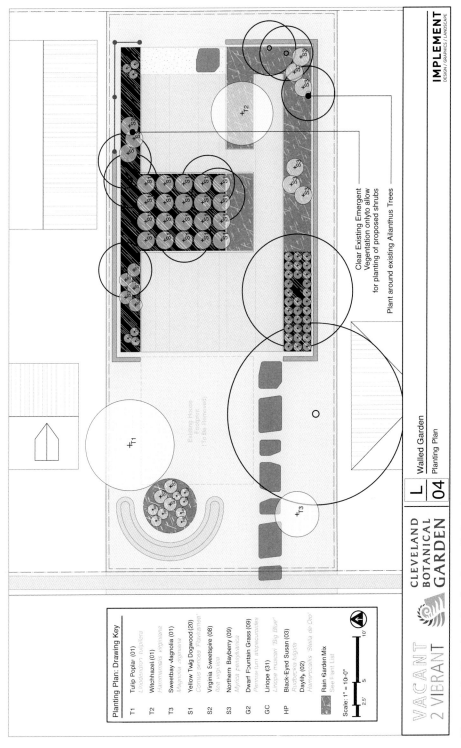

Figure A-5c. Planting plan for the walled garden site.

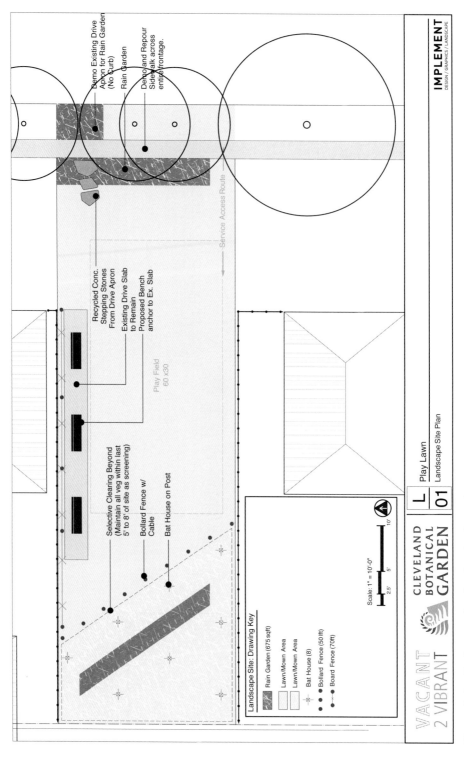

Figure A-6a. Site layout plan for the play lawn site.

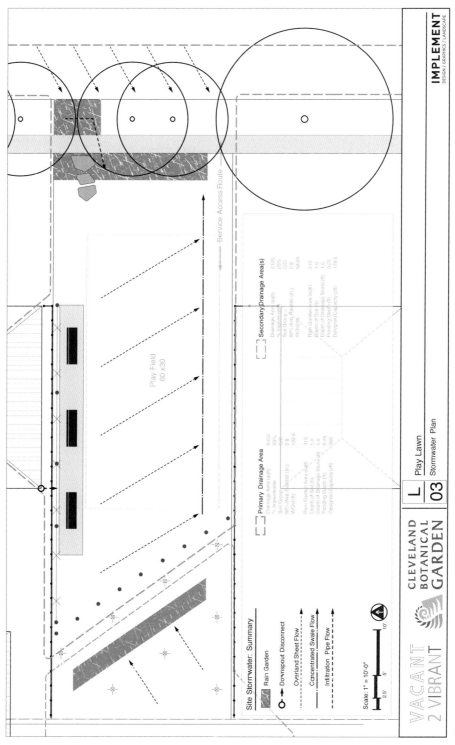

Figure A-6b. Stormwater management plan for the play lawn site.

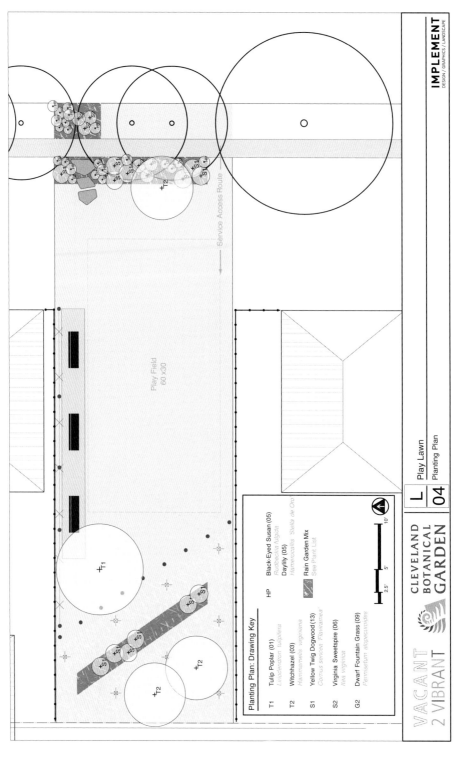

Figure A-6c. Planting plan for the play lawn site.

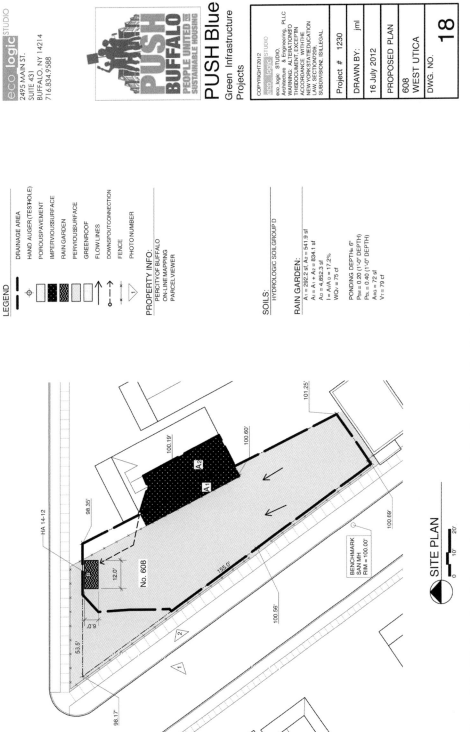

Figure A-7a. Site layout and stormwater management plan for the [outdoor] plant nursery site.

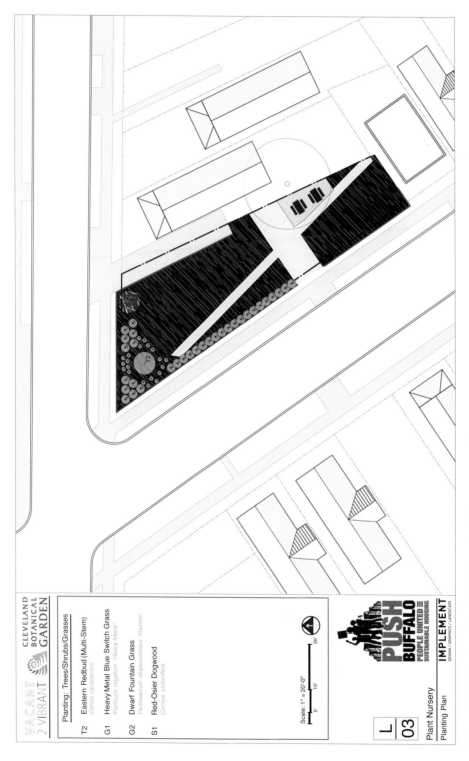

Figure A-7b. Planting plan for the [outdoor] plant nursery site.

Figure A-8a. Site layout plan for the handball court site.

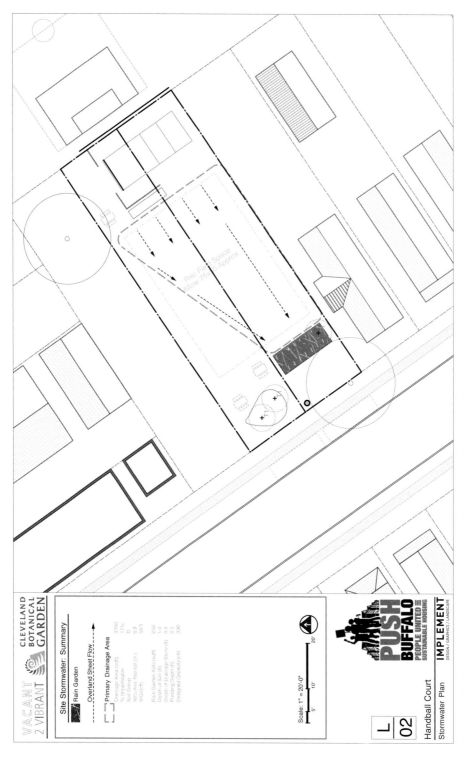

Figure A-8b. Stormwater management plan for the handball court site.

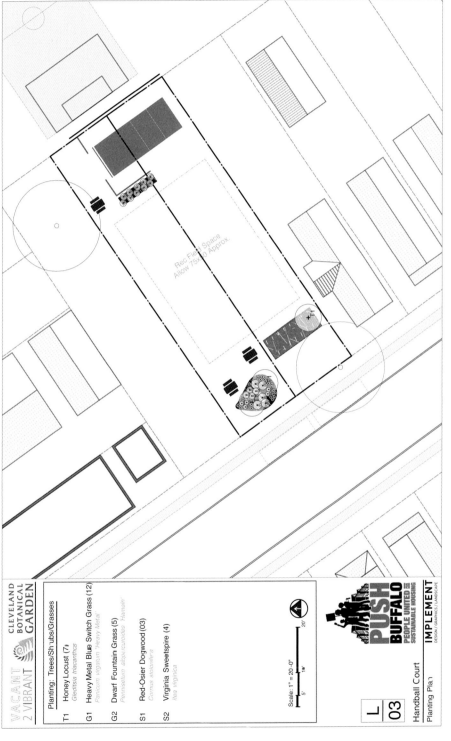

Figure A-8c. Planting plan for the handball court site.

170   Appendixz

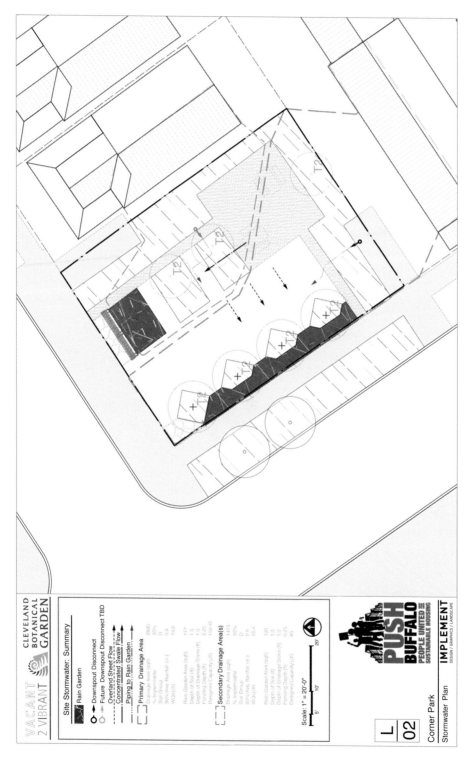

Figure A-9. Stormwater management plan for the corner park site.

Notes

Introduction

1. Mary M. Gardiner, Scott P. Prajzner, Caitlin E. Burkman, Sandra Albro, and Parwinder S. Grewal, "Vacant Land Conversion to Community Gardens: Influences on Generalist Arthropod Predators and Biocontrol Services in Urban Greenspaces," *Urban Ecosystems* 17, no. 1 (2014): 101–122.

2. Md Rumi Shammin, Walter E. Auch, and Laura Rose Brylowski, "Triple-Bottom-Line Analysis of Urban Agriculture as a Solution to Vacant Land Repurposing: A Case Study of Cleveland. A Report for Cleveland Botanical Garden for Great Lakes Protection Fund Project 949," Oberlin College, Oberlin, OH, November 2012, http://www.cbgarden.org/userfiles/files/Vacant-to-Vibrant/Benefits-of-Urban-Agriculture -White-Paper-2012.pdf

3. Many demolition contractors used poor-quality soil for backfill, as minimum standards for organic material and other soil components did not become common until recent years.

4. Brian C. Chaffin, William D. Shuster, Ahjond S. Garmestani, Brooke Furio, Sandra L. Albro, Mary Gardiner, MaLisa Spring, and Olivia Odom Green, "A Tale of Two Rain Gardens: Barriers and Bridges to Adaptive Management of Urban Stormwater in Cleveland, Ohio," *Journal of Environmental Management* 183 (2016): 431–441.

Chapter 1

1. Diana E. Bowler, Lisette Buyung-Ali, Teri M. Knight, and Andrew S. Pullin, "Urban Greening to Cool Towns and Cities: A Systematic Review of the Empirical Evidence," *Landscape and Urban Planning* 97, no. 3 (2010): 147–155.

2. Andrew Chee Keng Lee, Hannah C. Jordan, and Jason Horsley, "Value of Urban Green Spaces in Promoting Healthy Living and Wellbeing: Prospects for Planning," *Risk Management and Healthcare Policy* 8 (2015): 131.

3. Charles C. Branas, Eugenia South, Michelle C. Kondo, Bernadette C. Hohl, Philippe Bourgois, Douglas J. Wiebe, and John M. MacDonald, "Citywide Cluster Randomized Trial to Restore Blighted Vacant Land and Its Effects on Violence, Crime, and Fear," *Proceedings of the National Academy of Sciences* 115, no. 12 (2018): 2946–2951.

4. National Recreation and Park Association, *Creating Mini-Parks for Increased Physical Activity, Issue Brief* (Ashburn, VA: National Recreation and Park Association, n.d.).

5. Great Lakes Protection Fund, projects 949 and 949.01.

6. Ontario Ministry of Finance, *Ontario Population Projections Update, 2017–2041* (Oshawa, ON: Ontario Ministry of Finance, Spring 2018).

7. Luke J. Juday, *The Changing Shape of American Cities* (Charlottesville, VA: University of Virginia, February 2015).

8. Sylvie Fol and Emmanuèle C. Cunningham-Sabot, "Urban Decline and Shrinking Cities: A Critical Assessment of Approaches to Urban Shrinkage," *Annales de Géographie* 674 (2010): 359–383.

9. US Census Bureau, *Decennial Census of Population and Housing* (Suitland, MD: US Census Bureau, 1970 and 2010).

10. Ann O. Bowman and Michael A. Pagano, *Terra Incognita: Vacant Land and Urban Strategies* (Washington, DC: Georgetown University Press, 2004).

11. Fol and Cunningham-Sabot, "Urban Decline and Shrinking Cities"; Sigrun Kabisch, Annegret Haase, and Dagmar Haase, "Beyond Growth: Urban Development in Shrinking Cities as a Challenge for Modeling Approaches," *International Congress on Environmental Modelling and Software* 55 (July 2006), https://scholarsarchive.byu.edu /iemssconference/2006/all/55.

12. Maps throughout this book were created using ArcGIS software by Esri. ArcGIS and ArcMap are the intellectual property of Esri and are used herein under license. Copyright Esri. All rights reserved. http://www.esri.com.

13. Cleveland Neighborhood Progress, *Re-Imagining Cleveland: Vacant Land Re-Use Pattern Book* (Kent, OH: Cleveland Urban Design Collaborative, Kent State University, 2009).

14. US Department of Housing and Urban Development, "Temporary Urbanism: Alternative Approaches to Vacant Land," *Evidence Matters* (Winter 2014).

15. City of Chicago, *CitySpace: An Open Space Plan for Chicago* (Chicago, IL: City of Chicago, January 1998).

16. Pittsburgh City Planning, *OpenSpacePGH: Optimizing Pittsburgh's Open Space, Parks, and Recreation System* (Pittsburgh, PA: Pittsburgh City Planning, 2013).

17. Baltimore Department of Planning, *Baltimore Green Network Plan* (Baltimore, MD: Baltimore Department of Planning, 2018).

18. City of Gary Redevelopment Commission, *Request for Qualifications: 2018 Comprehensive Plan Update* (Gary, IN: City of Gary, 2017).

19. US Environmental Protection Agency (USEPA), *Report to Congress: Impacts and Control of CSOs and SSOs*, Report EPA 833-R-04-001 (Washington, DC: USEPA, 2004).

20. Combined sewer systems collect stormwater and sanitary discharges in the same pipes. During periods of wet weather, when flow exceeds the capacity of water treatment facilities, untreated water is discharged into waterways via combined sewer overflows, contributing to water pollution problems.

21. USEPA, "Combined Sewer Overflows (CSOs)," National Pollutant Discharge Elimination Systems (NPDES), accessed July 31, 2018, http://www.epa.gov/npdes/combined -sewer-overflows-csos.

22. Steven B. Johnson, *The Ghost Map: The Story of London's Most Terrifying Epidemic—and How It Changed Science, Cities, and the Modern World* (New York: Riverhead Books, 2006).

23. International Joint Commission, *14th Biennial Report on Great Lakes Water Quality* (Washington, DC: International Joint Commission Office, 2009).

24. "What Is Green Infrastructure?" Green Infrastructure, USEPA, accessed July 30, 2018, http://www.epa.gov/green-infrastructure/what-green-infrastructure.

25. *USEPA and State of Ohio v. Northeast Ohio Regional Sewer District*, case 1:10-cv-02895-DCN (6th Cir. 2011); NEORSD, *Appendix 3 Green Infrastructure Anticipated Co-benefits Analysis* (Cleveland, OH: NEORSD, March 26, 2015).

26. NEORSD, *Green Infrastructure Plan* (Cleveland, OH: NEORSD, April 23, 2012).

27. The Detroit Works Project Long Term Planning Steering Committee, *Detroit Future City: 2012 Detroit Strategic Framework Plan* (Detroit, MI: Detroit Future City, 2012).

28. Charles C. Branas, Rose A. Cheney, John M. MacDonald, Vicky W. Tam, Tara D. Jackson, and Thomas R. Ten Have, "A Difference-in-Differences Analysis of Health, Safety, and Greening Vacant Urban Space," *American Journal of Epidemiology* 174, no. 11 (2011): 1296–1306.

29. Susan Wachter, *The Determinants of Neighborhood Transformation in Philadelphia: Identification and Analysis: The New Kensington Pilot Study* (Philadelphia, PA: University of Pennsylvania, Wharton School, 2004).

30. Michelle C. Kondo, Sarah C. Low, Jason Henning, and Charles C. Branas, "The Impact of Green Stormwater Infrastructure Installation on Surrounding Health and Safety," *American Journal of Public Health* 105, no. 3 (2015): e114–e121.

31. Austin Troy, J. Morgan Grove, and Jarlath O'Neil-Dunne, "The Relationship between Tree Canopy and Crime Rates across an Urban–Rural Gradient in the Greater Baltimore Region," *Landscape and Urban Planning* 106, no. 3 (2012): 262–270.

32. "About Us," i-Tree, US Department of Agriculture Forest Service, accessed October 30, 2018, http://www.itreetools.org/about.php.

33. Nature Conservancy, *Funding Trees for Health: An Analysis of Finance and Policy Actions to Enable Tree Planting for Public Health* (Arlington, VA: The Nature Conservancy, 2017).

Chapter 2

1. Olivia B. Waxman, "Ellis Island's Busiest Day Ever Was 110 Years Ago. Here's Why," *Time*, April 17, 2017, http://time.com/4740248/ellis-island-busiest-day/.

2. Matthew E. Kahn, "The Silver Lining of Rust Belt Manufacturing Decline," *Journal of Urban Economics* 46, no. 3 (1999): 360–376.

3. Branas et al. "A Difference-in-Differences Analysis of Health, Safety, and Greening Vacant Urban Space"; Charles C. Branas, David Rubin, and Wensheng Guo, "Vacant Properties and Violence in Neighborhoods," *ISRN Public Health 2012* (2012): 1–23.

4. Mark Goldman, *High Hopes: The Rise and Decline of Buffalo, New York* (Albany, NY: SUNY Press, 1983).

5. US Census Bureau, *Decennial Census of Population and Housing* (Suitland, MD: US Census Bureau, 1970 and 2010).

6. "Architecture, Residential," *Encyclopedia of Cleveland History*, Case Western Reserve University, accessed July 30, 2018, http://case.edu/ech/articles/a/architecture-residential.

7. In 2014, the Cleveland Botanical Garden and the Holden Arboretum (of Kirtland, Ohio) merged to form Holden Forests & Gardens.

8. "Re-Imagining Cleveland," Cleveland Neighborhood Progress, accessed July 30, 2018, http://www.clevelandnp.org/reimagining-cleveland.

9. Cleveland City Planning Commission, *8 Ideas for Vacant Land Reuse in Cleveland* (Cleveland, OH: City of Cleveland, 2011).

10. *USEPA and State of Ohio v. Northeast Ohio Regional Sewer District*, case 1:10-cv-02895-DCN (6th Cir. 2011); NEORSD, *Appendix 3 Green Infrastructure Anticipated Co-benefits Analysis* (Cleveland, OH: NEORSD, March 26, 2015).

11. "Northeast Ohio Regional Sewer District Clean Water Act Settlement," USEPA, accessed July 30, 2018, http://www.epa.gov/enforcement/northeast-ohio-regional-sewer-district-clean-water-act-settlement.

12. Andrew Hurley, *Environmental Inequalities: Class, Race, and Industrial Pollution in Gary, Indiana, 1945–1980* (Chapel Hill, NC: University of North Carolina Press, 1995).

13. Hurley, *Environmental Inequalities.*

14. *USEPA and State of Indiana v. The City of Gary, Indiana, and Gary Sanitary District*, case 2:16-cv-00512 (7th Cir. 2016).

15. "Gary Comprehensive Plan Update," City of Gary Redevelopment Commission, accessed October 31, 2018, http://www.garyredev.org/compplan2018.html.

16. Goldman, *High Hopes.*

17. Diana Dillaway, *Power Failure: Politics, Patronage, and the Economic Future of Buffalo, New York* (Westminster, MD: Prometheus Books, 2006).

18. Goldman, *High Hopes.*

19. Goldman, *High Hopes.*

20. *Evapotranspiration* is the combination of *evaporation*, water lost directly into the air, and *transpiration*, water that is moved through plant roots and evaporated into the atmosphere through leaves and stems.

21. USEPA, "EPA Approves Buffalo Sewer Authority's Plan to Reduce Sewage and Water Pollution in Niagara River" (news release), April 14, 2014, https://archive.epa.gov/epapages/newsroom_archive/newsreleases/f62f59fbdaee3abd85257cba005a497e.html.

22. "Water Equity Clearinghouse: PUSH Buffalo," US Water Alliance, accessed October 30, 2018, http://uswateralliance.org/organization/push-buffalo.

23. Sandra L. Albro, Sean Burkholder, and Joseph Koonce, "Mind the Gap: Tools for a Parcel-Based Storm Water Management Approach," *Landscape Research* 42, no. 7 (2017): 747–760.

Chapter 3

1. Alexandra Dapolito Dunn, "Siting Green Infrastructure: Legal and Policy Solutions to Alleviate Urban Poverty and Promote Healthy Communities," *Boston College Environmental Affairs Law Review* 37, no. 1 (2010): 41–66.

2. US Census Bureau, 2010 Census Summary File 1 (SF1) and 2011 American Community Survey (ACS) databases.

3. New York State Department of Environmental Conservation, *New York State Stormwater Management Design Manual* (Albany, NY: New York State, January 2015).

4. City of Albany, *Albany 2030: The City of Albany Comprehensive Plan* (Albany, NY: City of Albany, 2011).

5. Charles C. Branas, Eugenia South, Michelle C. Kondo, Bernadette C. Hohl, Philippe Bourgois, Douglas J. Wiebe, and John M. MacDonald, "Citywide Cluster Randomized Trial to Restore Blighted Vacant Land and Its Effects on Violence, Crime, and Fear," *Proceedings of the National Academy of Sciences* 115, no. 12 (2018): 2946–2951

6. An additional factor influencing resident expectations about Vacant to Vibrant's projects may have been the manicured gardens of the Cleveland Botanical Garden, where project leadership was based.

Chapter 4

1. Title II of the Americans with Disabilities Act requires that governments make programs and services accessible to persons with disabilities. This applies to all programs but is not frequently discussed with regard to urban greening projects.

2. Will Allen and Charles Wilson, *The Good Food Revolution: Growing Healthy Food, People, and Communities* (New York: Avery Publishing, 2013).

Chapter 5

1. Brian C. Chaffin, Theresa M. Floyd, Sandra L. Albro, manuscripts in review, 2019.

2. Caroline Keicher, *Commercial Energy Policy Toolkit: Green Workforce Development*, fact sheet (Denver, CO: ICLEI – Local Governments for Sustainability – USA, 2011).

3. Noah Enelow and Chris Schildt, *Jobs & Equity in the Urban Forest* (Portland, OR: Ecotrust, 2017).

4. "High-road" businesses value employees and their communities as essential to businesses' financial success and advocate for fair pay and good benefits. American Sustainable Business Council, *Principles of High Road Employers: A Path to Building a Sustainable Economy* (Washington, DC: American Sustainable Business Council, 2018).

5. Zoë Roller, *An Equitable Water Future: Opportunities for the Great Lakes Region* (Washington, DC: US Water Alliance, 2018).

6. Alan Mallach, Ken Steif, and Kim Graziani, *The Re-Imagining Cleveland Vacant Lot Greening Program: Evaluating Economic Development and Public Safety Outcomes* (Washington, DC: Center for Community Progress, 2016).

7. Paul H. Gobster, Joan I. Nassauer, Terry C. Daniel, and Gary Fry. "The Shared Landscape: What Does Aesthetics Have to Do with Ecology?" *Landscape Ecology* 22, no. 7 (2007): 959–972.

Chapter 6

1. Clarence N. Stone, Robert P. Stoker, et al., *Urban Neighborhoods in a New Era: Revitalization Politics in the Postindustrial City* (Chicago: University of Chicago Press, 2015).

2. Allison H. Roy, Seth J. Wenger, Tim D. Fletcher, Christopher J. Walsh, Anthony R. Ladson, William D. Shuster, Hale W. Thurston, and Rebekah R. Brown, "Impedi-

ments and Solutions to Sustainable, Watershed-Scale Urban Stormwater Management: Lessons from Australia and the United States," *Environmental Management* 42, no. 2 (2008): 344–359.

3. Sandra L. Albro and Joseph F. Koonce, manuscript in preparation, 2018.

4. Average stormwater management per year made use of 30-year precipitation averages for the three cities from the National Weather Service.

5. NEORSD, *Green Infrastructure Plan* (Cleveland, OH: NEORSD, 2012).

6. Roy et al., "Impediments and Solutions to Sustainable, Watershed-Scale Urban Stormwater Management."

7. Luke M. Brander and Mark J. Koetse, "The Value of Urban Open Space: Meta-Analyses of Contingent Valuation and Hedonic Pricing Results," *Journal of Environmental Management* 92, no. 10 (2011): 2763–2773.

8. Cleveland Tree Coalition, *Reforesting the Forest City: The Cleveland Tree Canopy Goal* (Cleveland, OH: Cleveland Tree Coalition, 2018).

9. Hale W. Thurston, ed., *Economic Incentives for Stormwater Control* (Boca Raton, FL: CRC Press, 2011).

10. Hale W. Thurston, Haynes C. Goddard, David Szlag, and Beth Lemberg, "Controlling Storm-water Runoff with Tradable Allowances for Impervious Surfaces," *Journal of Water Resources Planning and Management* 129, no. 5 (2003): 409–418.

11. Geoffrey H. Donovan, David T. Butry, Yvonne L. Michael, Jeffrey P. Prestemon, Andrew M. Liebhold, Demetrios Gatziolis, and Megan Y. Mao, "The Relationship between Trees and Human Health: Evidence from the Spread of the Emerald Ash Borer," *American Journal of Preventive Medicine* 44, no. 2 (2013): 139–145.

12. The Arbor Day Foundation's Community Canopy program, formerly Energy-Saving Trees.

13. Roy et al., "Impediments and Solutions to Sustainable, Watershed-Scale Urban Stormwater Management."

14. NEORSD, *Project Clean Lake: NEORSD Green Infrastructure Plan Consent Decree Requirement* (Cleveland, OH: NEORSD, n.d.)

15. NEORSD, *Green Infrastructure Plan.*

16. Joan Iverson Nassauer, *The Aesthetics of Horticulture: Neatness as a Form of Care* (Alexandria, VA: American Society for Horticultural Science, 1988).

17. Paul H. Gobster, Joan I. Nassauer, Terry C. Daniel, and Gary Fry. "The Shared Landscape: What Does Aesthetics Have to Do with Ecology?" *Landscape Ecology* 22, no. 7 (2007): 959–972.

18. Charles C. Branas, Rose A. Cheney, John M. MacDonald, Vicky W. Tam, Tara D. Jackson, and Thomas R. Ten Have, "A Difference-in-Differences Analysis of Health, Safety, and Greening Vacant Urban Space," *American Journal of Epidemiology* 174, no. 11 (2011): 1296–1306.; Eugenia Garvin, Charles Branas, Shimrit Keddem, Jeffrey Sellman, and Carolyn Cannuscio, "More Than Just an Eyesore: Local Insights and Solutions on Vacant Land and Urban Health," *Journal of Urban Health* 90, no. 3 (2013): 412–426.

19. Gobster et al., "The Shared Landscape"; Joan Iverson Nassauer, Zhifang Wang, and

Erik Dayrell, "What Will the Neighbors Think? Cultural Norms and Ecological Design," *Landscape and Urban Planning* 92, no. 3–4 (2009): 282–292.

20. Shari L. Rodriguez, M. Nils Peterson, and Christopher J. Moorman, "Does Education Influence Wildlife Friendly Landscaping Preferences?" *Urban Ecosystems* 20, no. 2 (2017): 489–496.

21. P. Wesley Schultz, Jessica M. Nolan, Robert B. Cialdini, Noah J. Goldstein, and Vladas Griskevicius, "The Constructive, Destructive, and Reconstructive Power of Social Norms," *Psychological Science* 18, no. 5 (2007): 429–434.

22. Todd Makse and Anand E. Sokhey, "The Displaying of Yard Signs as a Form of Political Participation," *Political Behavior* 36, no. 1 (2014): 189–213.

23. Larissa Larsen and Sharon L. Harlan, "Desert Dreamscapes: Residential Landscape Preference and Behavior," *Landscape and Urban Planning* 78, no. 1–2 (2006): 85–100.

24. Jennifer R. Wolch, Jason Byrne, and Joshua P. Newell, "Urban Green Space, Public Health, and Environmental Justice: The Challenge of Making Cities 'Just Green Enough,'" *Landscape and Urban Planning* 125 (2014): 234–244.

25. National Institute of Realtors, *NAR 2017 Community Preference Survey* (Washington, DC: National Institute of Realtors, 2017).

26. Christine Haaland and Cecil Konijnendijk van den Bosch, "Challenges and Strategies for Urban Green-Space Planning in Cities Undergoing Densification: A Review," *Urban Forestry & Urban Greening* 14 (2015): 760–771.

27. "ParkScore 2018: Methodology," Trust for Public Land, accessed July 31, 2018, https://parkscore.tpl.org/methodology.php.

28. Philadelphia Water Department, *Green City, Clean Waters: Implementation and Adaptive Management Plan. Consent Order & Agreement Deliverable I* (Philadelphia, PA: Philadelphia Water Department, 2011).

29. New York State Department of Environmental Conservation, *2016 Open Space Conservation Plan* (New York: New York State, 2016).

Acknowledgments

Vacant to Vibrant required the collaborative work of a large number of people and organizations over several years. I am very grateful for their investment of time and energy.

I owe much appreciation to the Vacant to Vibrant core team, who helped coordinate all aspects of work in the three cities. Ryan Mackin gathered community feedback, provided general support, and created written reports that underlie several sections of this book.

I have been very fortunate to benefit from the expertise and mentorship generously provided by Joseph Koonce and Patti Barz during the hundreds of volunteer hours they donated to the project. I am similarly indebted to Geri Unger, who shaped and led early stages of Vacant to Vibrant. Joseph Koonce provided essential additional technical oversight for ecological monitoring, as well as written materials and ideas that also contributed to this book.

As city team leaders, Brenda Scott Henry at the City of Gary and Jenifer Kaminsky at the Buffalo Neighborhood Stabilization Corporation were instrumental to all aspects of Vacant to Vibrant's work in Gary and Buffalo—I greatly appreciate their years of collaboration.

Many thanks to project designers Sean Burkholder and Jason Kentner, who translated ideas and community feedback into artwork and design plans that are the embodiment of Vacant to Vibrant; and for the Buffalo projects, much appreciation for additional design and implementation support from Joshua Smith at People United for Sustainable Housing.

Financial support for Vacant to Vibrant was generously provided by the Great Lakes Protection Fund (projects 949 and 949.01). Shannon Donley smoothed many creases, and pointed questions from her, Amy Elledge, and J. David Rankin refined and expanded the reach of the project.

In Gary, I owe additional thanks to the residents of the Aetna neighborhood and

179

to Mayor Karen Freeman-Wilson, Deb Backhus, Martin Brown, Jewel Cody, Joseph Van Dyk, Cedric Kuykendall and the Urban Conservation Team, and Gayle Van Sessen. In Buffalo, I am grateful to colleagues at People United for Sustainable Housing, including PUSH Blue team members, as well as to the residents of the West Side. In Cleveland, Vacant to Vibrant was shaped by ongoing participation of residents of Crestwood, Shale, and Hulda Avenues, and by Jacqueline Gillon and colleagues at the Western Reserve Land Conservancy, Mike Supler, Nancy Boylan, Monroe Bynum, and Ted Auch, with additional maintenance support from Saint Luke's Foundation.

I am grateful to Island Press for the opportunity to publish these findings, and in particular to editor Courtney Lix, who saw potential in the project as a book and whose guidance and feedback about structure and flow helped it take form; and to Sharis Simonian for guidance throughout production.

Index